9/7/04
$12.00
B&T

A5

Withdrawn

Grand Canyon Place Names

D0038886

GRAND CANYON
PLACE NAMES

Gregory McNamee

Johnson Books
BOULDER

Published by Johnson Books, a division of Johnson Publishing Company, 1880 South 57th Court, Boulder, Colorado 80301. Visit our website at www.JohnsonBooks.com. E-mail: books@jpcolorado.com.

9 8 7 6 5 4 3 2 1

Cover design: Debra B. Topping
Cover photo by Gregory McNamee

Library of Congress Cataloging-in-Publication Data
McNamee, Gregory.
    Grand Canyon place names / Gregory McNamee.—2nd ed.
        p. cm.
    Includes bibliographical references.
    ISBN 1-55566-334-6
    1. Names, Geographical — Arizona — Grand Canyon National Park.
2. Names, Geographical — Arizona — Grand Canyon. 3. Grand
Canyon National Park (Ariz.) — History, Local. 4. Grand Canyon
(Ariz.) — History, Local. I. Title.
    F788.M3 2004
    917.91'32'300 — dc22   2003027953

Printed in the United States by
Johnson Printing
1880 South 57th Court
Boulder, Colorado 80301

Printed on ECF paper with soy ink

CONTENTS

Introduction 7

Grand Canyon Place Names A to Z 15

Bibliography 121

Head of the Grand Canyon, etching circa 1869

INTRODUCTION

One generation passes away,
and another generation comes:
but the earth abides forever.
Ecclesiastes 1:4

Language, Ralph Waldo Emerson once remarked, is "fossil poetry." Each word carries the accretions of its history, thicker than rings on an old tree. As languages constantly evolve, words change in time to convey meanings much different from their original intent. Consider, for instance, the changing fortunes of the English word *silly*, which once meant "soulful," then "happy," then something like "blissful," and eventually "foolish"—the logical conclusion, one supposes, of being blissed out. In our time, words come and go, shedding earlier connotations and acquiring new ones: we have only to think of fluid terms like *disk*, *gay*, *groovy*, and *bad* to understand why it seems that dictionaries are out of date the instant they're published.

Place names are also a kind of fossil poetry, but, once affixed to a map, they tend to change rather less, and rather more slowly, than do other kinds of words. Because of this conservative quality, they afford a kind of folk history, a snapshot in time that enables us to read in them a record of important events and to reconstruct something of the culture of the namers at the time they assigned names to the places they saw. The United States, with something like 3.5 million place names on its map, is singularly rich in this history. As the Scottish writer and traveler Robert Louis Stevenson notes in *Across the Plains*, "there is no part of the world where nomenclature is so rich, poetical, humorous, and picturesque. . . . There are few poems with a nobler music for the ear; a songful, tuneful land."

Those names, Duncan Emrich observes in *Folklore on the American Land*, break into predictable categories: the surnames of founders and settlers or of historical or otherwise important personages; English place names of the Old World; "foreign names," including those from imported faiths; classical and ancient names; names based on physical geography; names based on flora and fauna; names based on unusual or noteworthy incidents; and Native American names. In the Grand Canyon today, almost all of Emrich's categories obtain. Not so long ago, however, only a few of them did. When another Scottish writer, the great naturalist John Muir, came to the Canyon in 1902, he could write truly, "As yet, few of the promontories or throng of mountain buildings in the cañon are named. Nor among such exuberance of forms are names to be thought of by the bewildered, hurried tourist. He would be as likely to think of names for waves in a storm." A few years later the humorist Irvin S. Cobb, with an unwitting nod to Muir's birthplace, rejoined, "If these mountains were in Scotland, Sir Walter Scott and Bobby Burns would have written about them and they would be world-famous, and tourists from America would come and climb their slopes, and stand upon their tops, and sop up romance through all their pores. But being in Arizona, dwarfed by heaven-reaching ranges and groups that wall them in north, south, and west, they have not even a Christian name to answer to."

Since Muir's time, a flurry of naming has occurred in the Canyon. The Canyon is some 6 million years old; it has been inhabited for only a few thousand years, and inhabited by Anglo-Americans, those with the political power necessary to assign names and create maps, for just over a century. The power to name is in this instance part of a larger authority: Grand Canyon National Park was created as a federal holding in 1919. (The park is now some 277 miles long by 5 to 18 miles wide and comprises about 1,218,375 acres, or 1,900 square miles.) Most of the significant geographical features in the national park have been given formal designations, but the process is ongoing. Even in the 1990s, new names are being given to once-named or previously uncatalogued features (see, for example, the entry for Roosevelt Point).

Some of that naming is of the "folk" variety, with the contributions and perceptions of longtime residents figuring in the Grand Canyon's place names. John Wesley Powell (1834–1902), the heroic Civil War officer who, after losing an arm at the Battle of Shiloh, made two journeys down the Colorado River through the Grand Canyon, is responsible for many of these: to him we owe the names of Bright Angel Creek, Vaseys Paradise, Lava Falls, and dozens of other points on the map, including that of the Grand Canyon itself. Powell's companions and successors, men like Clarence Dutton (see Dutton Point) and Frederick Dellenbaugh (see Diamond Canyon), added much to Powell's roster. So did those who followed them, especially federal employees working for the National Park Service or the United States Geological Survey, employees whose names appear in such places as Sturdevant Point, Demaray Point, and Mather Point.

Much later naming, as you will see, shunned local terminology in favor of exotic imports honoring the gods and heroes of many nations and cultures. Little of it addresses issues of local physical geography: thus the map of the Grand Canyon contains names like Walhalla Plateau, Wotans Temple, Cheops Pyramid, Vishnu Temple, Ariel Point, names uprooted and replanted far from their homelands. According to a February 14, 1933 letter from Frederick Dellenbaugh to writer and historian Will Croft Barnes, this pattern of exotic naming was introduced by Clarence Dutton, who did not like Indian names, thinking them ugly, and who began naming points in the Grand Canyon after figures in world literature and religion. "I had several arguments with him on the subject as I objected violently to Oriental and Egyptian nomenclature," Dellenbaugh wrote. "I have continued to object ever since." Many others have objected to the presence of so many nonindigenous names as well, although, as Canyon historian J. Donald Hughes sensibly suggests, "perhaps it is better for the wonder of the world to bear the names of gods and heroes of every nation rather than the names of local miners, or American Indian names which were not applied by the Indians themselves, or purely descriptive names such as Red

Butte or Cedar Mountain [*q.v.*], or American presidents whose names have been given to features everywhere in the United States."

Whatever the case, those exotic names have been a part of the Canyon for a century and more, and it is unlikely that matters will ever change. Indeed, in a curious way, those names now seem fitting, if only because the geography of the Canyon is so vast as to cause a sort of religious awe, even a silence—as when Koyukon Indian mothers instruct their children not to discuss the comparative merits or sizes of the mountains surrounding them because, as they say, "your mouths are too small." Our mouths are small indeed, but that has not kept us from studding the map of the Grand Canyon with hundreds of names honoring our scientists (Darwin, Tyndall, Lyell), our explorers (Powell, Ives, Dellenbaugh), our gods (the Trinity, Krishna, Thor). That we have not loaded the map with more names relating to the Grand Canyon's defining feature—its spectacular geology—may serve as unwitting tribute to the spirit of those Koyukon teachers, or as evidence of a curious kind of blindness to what is before us. In any event, it is not possible to understand the Canyon without some knowledge of its geological history, on which there are many good published books, some of which are listed in the bibliography.

"The Grand Canyon of the Colorado is a world in itself, and a great fund of knowledge is in store for the philosophic biologist whose privilege it is to study exhaustively the problems there presented," the ecologist C. Hart Merriam once observed. The same problems and rewards await the student of the Grand Canyon's history, and of its names, whose origins are often elusive—strangely so, given that most are so recent and should, one would think, have reasonably well-documented pedigrees. In such instances, instead of neatly packaged histories we have legends, sometimes faulty remembrance, and sources ever in conflict; and often what we are left with is merely a best guess among equally attractive—or equally unlikely—choices. In assembling the little essays that follow, I have tried to let the sources speak for themselves, identifying the authorship of names where it is known, as so often it is not.

This small book relates the origins of some 330 place names in Grand Canyon National Park and the immediately adjacent area as they are found on the United States Geological Survey map N3600-W1145/28 x 60, *Grand Canyon National Park and Vicinity.* I envision its being used as a pocket reference for readers who are curious about the name of a given place, but also as a discursive history of the Canyon's naming, organized alphabetically and lightly but usefully cross-referenced. References for all quotations, when not supplied in the text itself, can be found in the bibliography. Details about historical figures mentioned or quoted are either given in the text, using cross-references where necessary, or can be found using the sources listed in the bibliography. Read from start to finish, *Grand Canyon Place Names* offers, I believe, a more complete accounting of that history than is found in any other single source. Even so, not every Canyon place name is to be found in these pages. I have not, for instance, commented on some names that seem too obvious to merit discussion: as, for example, The Basin, a geological depression on the North Rim. Neither have I given a complete accounting of place names outside the national park boundaries. More complete coverage of such place names, particularly in the west to Lake Mead, can be found in Nancy Brian's book *River to Rim,* which is organized by location relative to the Colorado and is thus especially useful to river runners. I recommend it to students of Grand Canyon history and general visitors alike.

Thanks go to the Arizona Humanities Council and its executive director, Dan Shilling, for a small grant of assistance in preparing this book, and to the staffs of the libraries of Northern Arizona University and the University of Arizona for their help. I am also grateful for the counsel of my friend Scott Thybony, a Grand Canyon veteran who knows far more about the Big Ditch than I ever will, and for the example of professors A. Richard Diebold and Sigmund Eisner, who introduced me to the study of place names all those years ago.

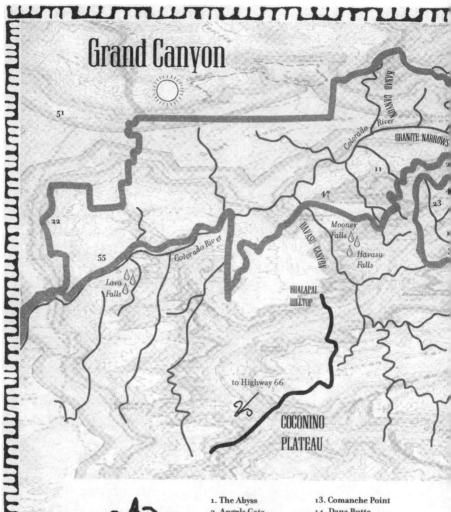

Grand Canyon

1. The Abyss
2. Angels Gate
3. Apache Point
4. Aztec Amphitheater
5. Brahma Temple
6. Cape Royal
7. Cape Solitude
8. Cárdenas Butte
9. Cedar Mountain
10. Cheops Pyramid
11. Chikapanagi Mesa
12. Chuar Butte
13. Comanche Point
14. Dana Butte
15. Darwin Plateau
16. De Motte Park
17. Desert View Point
18. Deva Temple
19. De Vaca Terrace
20. Diana Temple
21. Dutton Point
22. Emma, Mount
23. Fossil Canyon
24. Grandview Point

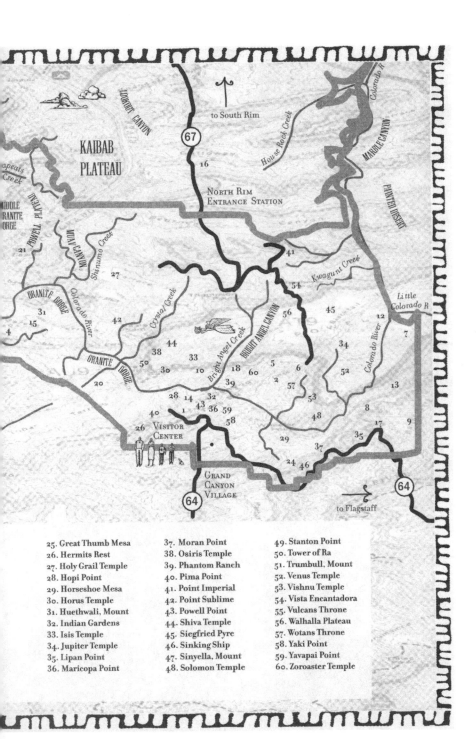

25. Great Thumb Mesa
26. Hermits Rest
27. Holy Grail Temple
28. Hopi Point
29. Horseshoe Mesa
30. Horus Temple
31. Huethwali, Mount
32. Indian Gardens
33. Isis Temple
34. Jupiter Temple
35. Lipan Point
36. Maricopa Point

37. Moran Point
38. Osiris Temple
39. Phantom Ranch
40. Pima Point
41. Point Imperial
42. Point Sublime
43. Powell Point
44. Shiva Temple
45. Siegfried Pyre
46. Sinking Ship
47. Sinyella, Mount
48. Solomon Temple

49. Stanton Point
50. Tower of Ra
51. Trumbull, Mount
52. Venus Temple
53. Vishnu Temple
54. Vista Encantadora
55. Vulcans Throne
56. Walhalla Plateau
57. Wotans Throne
58. Yaki Point
59. Yavapai Point
60. Zoroaster Temple

THE GEOLOGIC TIME SCALE

Era	Period	Millions of Years Ago
Cenozoic	Quaternary	0–1.6
	Tertiary	1.6–65
Mesozoic	Cretaceous	65–135
	Jurassic	135–205
	Triassic	205–250
Paleozoic	Permian	250–290
	Pennsylvanian	290–325
	Mississippian	325–355
	Devonian	355–410
	Silurian	410–438
	Ordovician	438–510
	Cambrian	510–570
Precambrian	Upper	570–2,500
	Lower	2,500–4,500

Adapted from Donald L. Baars, *Navajo Country: A Geology and Natural History of the Four Corners Region* (Albuquerque: University of New Mexico Press, 1995), xiii. Used with permission.

GRAND CANYON PLACE NAMES

THE ABYSS

The whole of the Grand Canyon might bear the descriptive name of this 6,884-foot headwall of Monument Creek, from the region of which, writes C. A. Higgins in his *Grand Cañon of the Colorado River* (1897), "twenty Yosemites might lie unperceived below." The point lies roughly midway between Grand Canyon Village and Hermits Rest.

As it is, it took some years before larger appellations were applied to the Canyon. When the Cárdenas party (*see* Cárdenas Butte) explored the area in 1540, its members referred to the great chasm before them simply as an "arroyo," a ditch different from others in the region only inasmuch as it was "several leagues wide." Even after exploring it for several days, Cárdenas would not believe the claim of his Indian guides that the river was half a league—more than a mile—across; he imagined its width to be only a few feet. (The true measure lies between these extremes.) Francisco Garcés, another Spanish explorer, called the Canyon *Puerto de Bucarelli*, after the viceroy of Spain. According to Frederick Dellenbaugh (*see* Diamond Canyon), the name *Grand Canyon* came into currency after 1872 thanks to John Wesley

Powell, the great explorer of the region (*see* Powell Plateau). The name was adopted by the United States Geographical Board to designate the area between the confluence of the Colorado and Little Colorado Rivers and the Grand Wash Cliffs.

AGATE CANYON

Richard T. Evans, a senior official of the United States Geographical Survey, named this deep central canyon in 1903 for the abundant agates found thereabouts. It is one of many canyons and rapids within Grand Canyon that bear the names of gemstones: others are Jasper, Jade, Quartz, Garnet, Turquoise, Emerald, Ruby, Sapphire, and Serpentine. With Agate Canyon, the last five canyons are collectively called The Jewels.

AKABA, MOUNT

An unnamed officer of the United States Geological Survey designated this 4,500-foot promontory after a Havasupai family of this name.

ALARCÓN TERRACE

Hernando de Alarcón (ca. 1515–1570), chamberlain to Viceroy Antonio de Mendoza of Mexico, commanded the flotilla that traveled up the east coast of the Gulf of California to support Francisco Vásquez de Coronado's land expedition (*see* Coronado Butte) in search of the fabled city of Cíbola.

On August 26, 1540, he reached the mouth of the Colorado, where, he reported in a letter to Mendoza, he found a "mighty river with so furious a current that we could scarcely sail against it." Alarcón named it the Buena Guía, "river of good guidance." Alarcón took a landing party upstream and made contact with Yuma and Cocopah Indians, whom he describes in his report to the viceroy, but he failed to make contact with Coronado. By virtue of this crossing, Alarcón deserves credit for being the first Spaniard to enter California. Alarcón returned to Mexico City, and in May 1541 he supported Coronado in a second expedition to find Cíbola. The maps he made on this journey helped establish the fact that California was not, as had been suspected, an island.

THE ALLIGATOR
Longtime Canyon resident Emery Kolb (1882–1976) thought this low ridge, stubbled with boulders, resembled the back of an alligator, and named it accordingly.

ALSAP BUTTE
John Alsap (1832–1886) was an early promoter of the Salt River Valley, and is sometimes referred to as the "father of Maricopa County" for his work there as a real estate attorney and judge. Frank Bond, another prominent citizen of Maricopa County and onetime chairman of the United States Board of Geographic Names, named this butte for Alsap in 1930. Although Bond is the author of many Grand Canyon place names, his own name does not yet appear on the map.

ANGELS GATE
The writer George Wharton James fancifully named this 6,761-foot butte, which lies below Wotans Throne (*q.v.*). The name makes a nice if accidental counterpoint to the equally fanciful, and appropriately lower, Hades Knoll at the far west end of the Canyon.

APACHE POINT
The United States Geographical Board designated this 6,322-foot West Rim point, lying above Apache Terrace and Elves Chasm, after the Apache Indians of Arizona and New Mexico. The Zuni word *apachu* means "enemy." The Apache refer to themselves variously as Indeh, Deneh, or Dene.

In *The Man Who Walked Through Time*, his memoir of hiking the Canyon, Colin Fletcher observes that the Apache Trail below this point, "though betraying no hint of human use, turned out to be a busy burro turnpike." Fletcher wrote in 1967. With increased visitation, human use has increased, but park rangers removed wild burros from the national park in 1976 and 1977.

APOLLO TEMPLE

Apollo, the son of Leto and Zeus, is the Greek god of prophecy, with aspects of agriculture and, like the Hindu god Shiva (*see* Shiva Temple), of disease and warfare. His name in Greek probably means "destroyer," although some scholars trace it to a verb, already extinct in classical times, meaning "to drive away." Apollo's haunts were river valleys and mountaintops, so his presence in the Canyon is not inappropriate. François Matthes (*see* Matthes Point) suggested this name in 1902.

ARIEL POINT

Ariel was a Moabite chief who figures briefly in the Biblical books of 2 Samuel and Chronicles. His name later appears as that of a sprite in Shakespeare's play *The Tempest* and of a fallen angel in Milton's *Paradise Lost*. In Hebrew, Ariel means "temple of God," a fitting name for this vista on the Walhalla Plateau (*q.v.*). François Matthes suggested the name.

ARROWHEAD TERRACE

Frank Bond (*see* Alsap Butte) named this spur between Stone Creek (*q.v.*) and Galloway Canyon (*q.v.*) because of its resemblance to a stone arrowhead.

ASBESTOS CANYON

Up until 1903, when 602 people died in Chicago's terrible Iroquois Theater Fire, entertainment halls tended to be rickety, dangerous, untended palaces of fun. New regulations requiring the installation of emergency exits and asbestos fire curtains kept similar disasters from befalling later theatergoers. With those regulations came a huge demand for asbestos, which the Canyon was known to contain in quantity. John Hance (*see* Hance Creek) had discovered an asbestos lode in this canyon in 1902 and mined it commercially for several years.

AWATOVI CREEK

Awatovi means "Bow People Clan lookout" in Hopi. Awatovi was one of the most ancient eastern Hopi pueblos, and reports of it appear in the journals of several conquistadors. In 1629 a Franciscan mission was founded there; its first priest, Padre Fray Porras, was murdered soon thereafter. Rebellious Hopis burned the pueblo to the ground in 1700. Its ruins were barely visible at the turn of this century, when Jesse Fewkes surveyed the site for excavations later conducted by the Peabody Museum in the 1930s.

AYER POINT

Emma Burbank Ayer, wife of the Flagstaff lumberer Edward Ayer, was the first known Anglo woman to enter the Canyon, traveling in 1885 down the Hance Trail, which skirts this point to the right of Hance Canyon.

AZTEC AMPHITHEATER

Many geographical features in the Southwest have been fancifully named *Aztec* after their antiquity, it having once been presumed that the Aztecs were the oldest New World civilization. This is not true: a dozen civilizations in Mexico alone antedate them. Neither is the joke, once popular among rangers as a reply to tourists' questions, that Aztecs built the Grand Canyon when they were done with their pyramids.

BADGER CREEK

What the writer George R. Stewart calls "incident names" pepper the American landscape: San Diego, California, was first sighted by Spanish explorers on the feast day of St.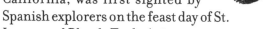
James, and Bloody Tank, Arizona, commemorates an American massacre of an Apache band. The names of animals are especially susceptible to these "events," as when a sow sighted in a mountain park lent its name to Colorado's Bear Lake, and a coyote loping across the Arizona Strip turned up in Wolf Hole, Arizona.

Badger Creek is one such place. According to Joseph Fish, a territorial historian, Mormon pioneer Jacob Hamblin shot a badger along its banks. The badger, Fish continues, "was carried to another creek and put on the fire to boil. In the morning, instead of stew, the alkali in the water and the fat from the badger had resulted in a kettle of soap," whence the origins of the name of nearby Soap Creek as well.

In his 1914 book *Through the Grand Canyon from Wyoming to Mexico*, Ellsworth Kolb writes of the rapids at Badger Creek,

> *It is difficult to describe the rapids with the foot-rule standard, and give an idea of their power. One unfamiliar with "white water" usually associates a twelve-foot descent or a ten-foot wave with a similar wave on the ocean. There is no comparison. The waters of the ocean rise and fall, the waves travel, the water itself, except in breakers, is comparatively still. In bad rapids the water is whirled through at the rate of ten or twelve miles an hour, in some cases much swifter; the surface is broken by streams shooting up from every submerged rock; the weight of the river is behind it, and the waves, instead of tumbling forward, quite as often break upstream. Such waves, less than six feet high, are often dangers to be shunned. After being overturned in them we learned their tremendous power, a power we would never have associated with any water, before such an experience, short of a waterfall.*

BANTA POINT

Pioneer historian and writer Will Croft Barnes named this promontory after A. F. Banta, chief scout for General Crook's command at Fort Whipple, near modern Prescott. Banta was born in Indiana in 1846 and christened with the name Charles A. Franklin. He came to Arizona in 1863, when he claimed to have discovered Meteor Crater. He served in various appointed and elected governmental positions and lived in several spots throughout the territory, changing names as he moved from place to place. There seems to have been nothing sinister in this, but it excited comment all the same as he went from Charles Franklin to A. F. Banta to C. A. Franklin to Charles Elbert Franklin, under which name he wrote the famed short story, "The Message to García." He finally settled on Albert Franklin Banta, the name by which he was known when he retired in Springerville at the turn of the century.

BARBENCITA BUTTE

This 4,699-foot rise just above Nankoweap Creek was named for the Navajo leader Barboncito (1820–1871), whose name means "little beard" in Spanish. The misspelling has not been corrected. Barboncito's Navajo name was Hastin (sometimes given as Hosteen) Daagii, and it was he who signed the treaty of 1868 that granted the Navajo people a reservation in Arizona, following several years of warfare and internment.

BASALT CREEK

Frank Bond (see Alsap Butte) named this intermittent stream after the basalt cliffs above it, part of the billion-year-old Cardenas Basalt complex of the Unkar Group.

BASS CAMP

William Wallace Bass was an explorer who came to the Canyon in 1883. According to a story told by the writer George Wharton James and repeated by historian Will Croft Barnes, a Havasupai Indian named Captain Burro led Bass to a point within the Canyon where Bass built his "camp." Bass paid Captain Burro a sack of flour and half a side of beef for the service. Bass later built a cable car at Mile 107.5. (For an explanation of the river mile system of measurement in the Canyon, *see* Lees Ferry *and* 140 Mile Canyon.) He operated it until his retirement in 1925, when he sold his Canyon holdings for $20,500. Writing in the *Geographical Review* of 1924, Claude Birdseye describes the cable car system: "At Bass Canyon rapids we passed under a cable ferry 300 feet long and 50 feet above water. The cable affords a fair crossing of the river at this point, and with a man on top of the car to operate the windlass, a horse can be carried across, if he is a tractable animal."

Bass was the author of much verse about the Canyon that, although without much literary merit, records many points of interest. One poem describes the Colorado River:

Oh! where did you come from, you dirty red thing,
Born in the mountains of many a spring
Whose clear crystal waters you claimed as your own,
Mixed them with mud and lashed them to foam?
First is the "Green," next is the "Grand,"
But now Colorado, because of your sand,
Your silt and your mud, and now do they say,
That out of pure spite you hid it away
In this unearthly, inaccessible place,
So that no man could find you, or look into your face,
Except it might be as he stood on your brink,
A half-league above you and died for a drink.

Bass Limestone, a feature of Canyon geology, was named after Bass. On his death in 1933, his ashes were scattered over Holy Grail Temple (*q.v.*).

Bass's son William, a chronicler of the Canyon, grew up at Bass Camp. "I was born in Williams, Arizona, July 26, 1900," he writes, "only missing being born at Bass Camp by one week, as it was necessary for my Mother to be taken to the nearest hospital and doctor. As soon as she could travel again, I was back at home on the Rim; so I say I was practically the first white child born on the Rim of the Grand Canyon. I also feel that I inherited the Grand

Canyon. . . . I was born with its magical spell in my veins. It was an important part of my parents' lives. It was my first impression of the world, my first realization of things about me."

THE BATTLESHIP
This ridge was named descriptively for its appearance at the time of the Spanish-American War, when battleships commonly figured in the news. (For a note on the appropriateness of such a name in the Grand Canyon, see Brahma Temple.) In a letter of 1914, the explorer and photographer Emery Kolb refers to this as Battleship Iowa Point, but this name does not appear in other sources.

BEALE POINT
Beale Point, which rises 6,400 feet on the Powell Plateau (q.v.), is named after Edward Fitzgerald Beale (1822–1893), a naval officer whose greatest military successes took place on dry land. An 1842 graduate of the United States Naval Academy, Beale served in California under Philip Kearney during the war with Mexico, receiving severe wounds at the battle of San Pasqual. With army scout Kit Carson, Beale later served as a transcontinental military messenger, bringing the first news to Washington of the 1848 California Gold Rush. Beale left the Navy in 1851, and was shortly afterward appointed general superintendent of Indian affairs for the departments of California and Nevada.

In 1856 Beale assumed command of the California state militia, during which service he created a camel corps for military transport in the desert Southwest, hiring drovers from the Near East to train and maintain the animals. In 1857 he began surveying a new overland route across southern New Mexico and Arizona, again using camels as pack animals. Beale retired from military service entirely after the Civil War, and in 1876 he served as United States ambassador to Austria-Hungary. Monuments to Beale and his colleagues grace several Arizona towns, notably Kingman and Quartzsite.

BEDIVERE POINT

In Arthurian legend, Bedivere was one of the original knights of the Round Table, and the only one to die in old age in his own home, the others having been driven into exile after Arthur's death. In Tennyson's *Morte d'Arthur*, Arthur relates the history of his kingship to Bedivere, his last loyal companion, lamenting the decline of his rule through treachery:

My house has been my doom
But call thou not this traitor of my house
Who hath dwelt beneath one roof with me.
My house are rather they who sware my vows,
Yea, even while they brake them.

Bedivere's reply predicts the resurrection of the court in the place names of the Grand Canyon:

For now I see the true old times are dead. . . .
And the days darken round me, and the years,
Among new men, strange faces, other minds.

According to historian C. M. Matthews, Arthurian place names have tended to live on in England even as the places they once marked come no longer to exist. "Because [Arthur] fought for the British people," he suggests, "it was natural that their descendants in the Celtic west remembered the places associated with him by their Celtic names rather than by new ones given by their enemies, the English." It is tempting to think that this attachment obtained among the mostly Scots-Irish American explorers, not far removed from the generation of the Revolutionary War, who named so many places in the Canyon. In this instance a man of Welsh descent, Richard T. Evans, gave 7,600-foot Bedivere Point its name.

BLACKTAIL CANYON

Frank Bond (*see* Alsap Butte) named this narrow canyon off Stephen Aisle for its abundant population of mule deer (*Odocoileus hemionus*), whose thin white tail ends in a dark tip. William Calvin rejoins in *The River That Flows Uphill* that the place is now "not known so much for blacktail deer as for a spectacular canyon of corrugated Tapeats Sandstone leading back up to Powell Plateau."

BOUCHER CREEK

Louis D. Boucher, a French-Canadian, arrived as a prospector in the Grand Canyon in 1891. He was dubbed "the Hermit" (*see* Hermit Basin) on account of his solitary ways, and in his solitude he carved out a little bit of paradise: alongside a trail he blazed from the South Rim to Dripping Springs and out to the river, he planted an orchard of seventy-five fruit trees, kept an ample and varied vegetable garden, and even built a few cabins to house visitors. He built and named Dripping Spring Trail. The small creek named for him comes into the Colorado River near a point on the Tonto Trail and is seldom more than a foot or two wide.

In 1913, the humorist Irvin S. Cobb visited the area and wrote of a like-minded solitary inhabitant,

You pass above the gloomy shadows . . .
and wind beneath a great box-shaped
formation of red sandstone set on a
spindle rock and balancing there in dizzy
space like Mohammed's coffin; and then,
at the end of a mile-long jog along a natural
terrace stretching itself mid-way between
Heaven and the other place, you come to
the residence of Shorty, the official hermit of the Grand Cañon.

Shorty is a little, gentle old man, with warped legs and
mild blue eyes and a set of whiskers of such indeterminate aspect
that you cannot tell at first look whether they are just coming out
or just going back in. He belongs—or did belong—to the vast van-
ishing race of oldtime gold prospectors. Halfway down the trail

he does light housekeeping under an accommodating flat ledge that pouts out over the pathway like a snuffdipper's under lip. He has a hole in the rock for his chimney, a breadth of weathered gray canvas for his door and an eight-mile stretch of the most marvelous panorama on earth for his front yard. He minds the trail and watches out for the big boulders that sometimes fall in the night; and, except in the tourist season, he leads a reasonably quiet existence.

Alongside of Shorty, Robinson Crusoe was a tenement-dweller, and Jonah, week-ending in the whale, had a perfectly uproarious time; but Shorty thrives on a solitude that is too vast for imagining. He would not trade jobs with the most potted potentate alive—only sometimes in midsummer he feels the need of a change stealing over him, and then he goes afoot out into the middle of Death Valley and spends a happy vacation of five or six weeks with the Gila monsters and the heat.

BOULDER CREEK
A descriptive name: the bed of this creek, near Lyell Butte *(q.v.)*, is choked with large boulders.

BOUNDARY RIDGE
The northern boundary of Grand Canyon National Park follows this 7,000-foot ridgeline, for which reason surveyor Richard T. Evans gave it this name.

BOURKE POINT
Arizona pioneer and historian Will Croft Barnes named this point for one of the most outstanding officers the United States Army ever produced, John Gregory Bourke (1846–1896). A Pennsylvanian, Bourke lied about his age to enlist in the Union Army, and won the Medal of Honor for gallantry in action at the Battle of Stone River when he was only sixteen. At the end of the Civil War Bourke entered the United States Military Academy and was commissioned a lieutenant of cavalry in 1869. Assigned to Fort Grant, Arizona, Bourke fought in the Apache wars under General George S. Crook, whose aide he became. He later served in

the Sioux and Cheyenne campaigns, returning to Arizona with Crook to battle against the Apache leader Geronimo. Bourke was an adept student of Indian cultures, and he wrote several ethnological volumes that are still valuable today, especially *The Snake Dance of the Moquis of Arizona* (1892). In his memoir *On the Border with Crook*, Bourke describes the South Rim and environs as he saw them in the early 1870s, when lumbering had already denuded much of the region:

> *Our line of march led through the immense pine forests, and to the right of the lofty snow-mantled peak of San Francisco, one of the most beautiful mountains in America. It seems to have been, at some period not very remote, a focus of volcanic disturbance, pouring out lava in inconceivable quantities, covering the earth for one hundred miles square, and to a depth in places of five hundred feet. This depth can be ascertained by any geologist who will take the trail out from the station of Ash Fork, on the present Atlantic and Pacific Railroad, and go north-northeast, to the Cataract Cañon, to the village of the Ava-Supais. In beginning the descent towards the Cataract Cañon, at the "Black Tanks," the enormous depth of the "flow" can be seen at a glance. What was the "forest primeval" at that time on the Mogollon has since been raided by the rapacious forces of commerce, and at one point—Flagstaff, favorably located in the timber belt—has since been established the great Ayers-Riordan saw and planing mill [see Ayer Point], equipped with every modern appliance for the destruction of the old giants whose heads had nodded in the breezes of centuries. Man's inhumanity to man is an awful thing. His inhumanity to God's beautiful trees is scarcely inferior to it. Trees are nearly human; they used to console man with their oracles, and I must confess my regret that the Christian dispensation has so changed the opinions of the world that the soughing of the evening wind through their branches is no longer a message of hope or a solace to sorrow.*

Bourke retired from the army in 1895 and died soon afterward. His papers are housed at the United States Military Academy at West Point, New York.

BOYSAG POINT

Boysag is the Havasupai word for bridge, perhaps referring to nearby rock arches instead of the artificial bridge on the trail leading to the point.

BRADLEY POINT

Frank Bond (*see* Alsap Butte) named this point for G. Y. Bradley, a boatman with the first Powell expedition into the Grand Canyon.

BRADY PEAK

Early in 1884, a dapper con man named James Addison Reavis wandered into the Phoenix courthouse and proclaimed himself to be the heir to 10,000 square miles of the Arizona Territory. As evidence Reavis produced a deed supposedly signed by King Ferdinand VI of Spain himself. In 1746, or so the story went, the king awarded Reavis's Mexican wife's ancestor Miguel de Peralta de Cordoba nearly the whole of Arizona from the banks of the Gila south, including dozens of mines and rich agricultural holdings. After deliberating for a short time, the territorial court decided that Reavis's claim was valid, and the self-styled Baron of Arizona set up shop at an old railroad watering station called Arizola. He merrily sold off portions of his estate to hundreds of its earlier owners, earning a fortune in the process. For twelve years Reavis lived a life of splendor, occasionally deigning to leave his mansion to drive about his fiefdom in an ornate carriage he had imported from England. As time passed, his regal arrogance earned him many enemies.

One was Tom Weedin, editor of the *Florence Citizen*, the region's leading newspaper. Weedin suspected a hoax from the start and wrote thundering editorials denouncing Reavis. In 1893 Weedin's printer went to Phoenix on a weekend holiday and, on a hunch, looked up the Peralta deed. He noticed that the supposedly ancient document was set in a typeface that had only recently been invented, and that another bore the watermark of a Wisconsin paper mill. Weedin reported these details in his paper, and Reavis's game was up. The Baron of Arizona was convicted of forgery in 1895 and was sentenced to six years in the New Mexico Territorial Prison in Santa Fe. The comparatively light term may have reflected the general mood of embarrassment that followed Weedin's discovery. (At about the same time, the courts uncovered a similar fraudulent land grant in California, supposedly giving title to most of the San Francisco Bay Area to one José Yves Limantour.) Paroled after two years, Reavis made his way to California, dying penniless in Los Angeles in 1914. His memory is enshrined in Samuel Fuller's 1950 feature film *The Baron of Arizona*, where a villainous Vincent Price chews up the scenery in the role of Reavis.

Peter R. Brady, a Tucsonan who came to Arizona after serving in the Mexican War, was a special agent in the Reavis case, and the evidence he amassed broke Reavis's claim once and for all. He later served in the Arizona legislature, and Frank Bond (*see* Alsap Butte) memorialized his good works by naming this 8,121-foot rise after him.

BRAHMA TEMPLE

Brahma is the creator aspect of the Hindu supreme Being; the destroyer aspect is Shiva (*see* Shiva Temple). This 7,553-foot bluff was named by Clarence Dutton (*see* Dutton Point).

Taking his part in the long-standing debate over exotic names in favor of indigenous ones (*see* Bedivere Point), Julius Stone remarks in his book *Canyon Country*, "By poetry men seek to express that which is intangible, which is beyond finite reach. 'The Battleship' [*q.v.*] may seem appropriate as the name of a butte near at hand and easily reached, but for the great, ornately carved, and gorgeously decorated structures which may not be readily reached and which to most people must remain distant, unattainable and shrouded in mystery, such names as the Tower of Ra, Buddha Temple,

Cheops Pyramid, Zoroaster Temple, Haunted Canyon, and Dragon Head seem pleasingly appropriate." Brahma Temple is just such a structure.

BREEZY POINT

Emery C. Kolb and Ellsworth Kolb, noted photographers and explorers of the Canyon, gave this Hermit Trail overlook below the South Rim its classically descriptive name because the winds there on several occasions kicked up enough gravel to obscure their view.

BRIDGERS KNOLL

Although he probably never saw the Grand Canyon, the famed mountain man James Bridger (1804–1881) is honored with the name of this small rise overlooking Surprise Valley (*q.v.*).

BRIGHT ANGEL CREEK

When the members of Major John Wesley Powell's (*see* Powell Plateau) geographical survey party guided their wooden boats down the Colorado River through the Grand Canyon in the summer of 1869, their leader had many opportunities to exercise his wide learning in natural and human history by naming the places they encountered. When they beached one evening at the confluence of a small stream far below what is now Grand Canyon Village, Powell seems to have been fresh out of ideas, for all he could come up with for the watercourse and its rugged canyon was Silver Creek. He soon recalled the lyrics of a hymn from his Methodist boyhood, however:

> *Shall we gather at the river,*
> *Where bright angel's feet have trod,*
> *With its crystal tide forever*
> *Flowing by the throne of God.*

And thereafter the stream, the canyon, and later the South Rim's most heavily used trail have been called Bright Angel—a nice counterbalance to the Dirty Devil River upstream (*q.v.*). Powell wrote of it in his journal entry for August 16, 1869, "The Colorado is never a clear stream, but for the past three or four days it has been raining much of the time, and the floods, which are pouring over the walls, have brought down great quantities of mud, making it exceedingly turbid now. The little affluent which we have discovered here, is a clear, beautiful creek or river, as it would be termed in this western country where streams are not abundant."

Powell's happy recollection also supplied Marguerite Henry with the name of the spry burro whose adventures she recounts in her beloved children's novel *Brighty of the Grand Canyon.*

BUDDHA TEMPLE

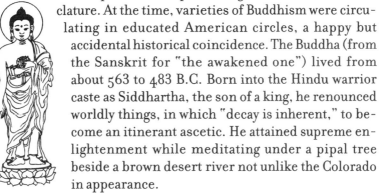

Henry Gannett, a surveyor for Clarence Dutton (*see* Dutton Point), named this 7,203-foot butte in 1906 in keeping with Dutton's penchant for preferring exotic to local nomenclature. At the time, varieties of Buddhism were circulating in educated American circles, a happy but accidental historical coincidence. The Buddha (from the Sanskrit for "the awakened one") lived from about 563 to 483 B.C. Born into the Hindu warrior caste as Siddhartha, the son of a king, he renounced worldly things, in which "decay is inherent," to become an itinerant ascetic. He attained supreme enlightenment while meditating under a pipal tree beside a brown desert river not unlike the Colorado in appearance.

BURRO CANYON

According to explorer Emery Kolb, this canyon was once overrun by wild burros, the offspring of stock introduced by prospectors. Even so, most sources suggest that the canyon was named for Captain Burro, a prominent Havasupai guide (*see* Bass Camp).

CAPE FINAL

Clarence Dutton (*see* Dutton Point) named this eastern point of the Walhalla Plateau (*q.v.*) in 1880, calling it, without elaboration, "doubtless the most interesting spot on the Kaibab."

CAPE ROYAL

Surveyor Clarence Dutton named this point, the southernmost extension of the Walhalla Plateau, in 1882, "because of its commanding site," according to historian Will Croft Barnes. It overlooks Wotans Throne (*q.v.*) and Vishnu Temple (*q.v.*).

Writing in 1913, Theodore Roosevelt described the view from Cape Royal:

> *From the southernmost point of this table-land the view of the canyon left the beholder solemn with the sense of awe. At high noon, under the unveiled sun, every tremendous detail leaped in glory to the sight; yet in hue and shape the change was unceasing from moment to moment. When clouds swept the heavens, vast shadows were cast; but so vast was the canyon that these shadows seemed patches of gray and purple and umber. The dawn and the evening twilight were brooding mysteries over the dusk of the abyss; night shrouded the immensity but did not hide it, and to none of the sons of men is it given to tell of the wonder and splendor of sunrise and sunset in the Grand Canyon of the Colorado.*

CAPE SOLITUDE

Overlooking the confluence of the Little Colorado and Colorado Rivers, this promontory was named by surveyor Clarence Dutton because, as he put it, "it stands solitary and alone."

CARBON BUTTE

Canyon surveyor Charles Walcott named this butte and the creek that flows below it for the seams of coal he found on the Coconino Plateau (*q.v.*). At the time of its naming, coal mining enjoyed a tremendous boom throughout the West; several towns, like Coalville, Utah, and Carbona, California, came into being then.

CÁRDENAS BUTTE

This mesa was named after Lieutenant López de Cárdenas, whom Francisco Coronado (see Coronado Butte) ordered to locate the great river that Don Pedro de Tovar (see Tovar Terrace) had reported on an earlier scouting expedition near the Hopi mesas. Cárdenas made his way to a point on the South Rim somewhere between Desert View and Moran Point, where he correctly judged the distance between the rims to be about ten miles. He also calculated the width of the river, however, to be only six feet, although his Hopi guides adamantly told him that he was wrong.

CASTOR TEMPLE

Castor and Pollux were the divine twins, the Dioscuri, of Greek mythology. This butte, along with Pollux Temple, flanks Sapphire Canyon below Piute Point. Fittingly, in ancient Rome the temple of the twins stood close by the temple of Vesta, as their temples do here in Grand Canyon.

CEDAR MOUNTAIN

This 7,057-foot elevation is forested with cedar (*Juniperus monosperma* and *osteosperma*), a ubiquitous tree on the Colorado Plateau. Willa Cather writes in *Death Comes for the Archbishop* that "every conical hill was spotted with smaller cones of juniper, a uniform yellowish green." The tree's berries formed an important part of the indigenous winter diet in years when pinyon nuts were scarce. Dyes made from its bark figure prominently in traditional Navajo textiles.

In *The Man Who Walked Through Time* Colin Fletcher observes,

> *Within a few miles of the South Rim of Grand Canyon stand two isolated and widely separated hills called Red Butte [q.v.] and Cedar Mountain. These hills, rising up from the same white limestone as forms the Canyon's Rim, are composed for the most part of clearly stratified red sandstones and shales. Almost identical rocks are still found throughout large areas to*

the north and east of Grand Canyon, and it seems certain that
they once formed a continuous layer over the whole region. Then
local conditions must have changed, just long enough for wind
and water to erase this topmost layer. The fragmentary but per-
suasive evidence that it once existed has been left behind at Red
Butte and Cedar Mountain by sheer chance: because the soft red
rocks that now form Red Butte were protected from erosion by a
layer of hard lava, and those of Cedar Mountain by pebble-rock.
Today, these protective layers still cap the hills.

CHEMEHUEVI POINT

The Chemehuevi Indians are indigenous to the lower Colorado
River. The name comes from the language of the Halchidoma
people, but the meaning is uncertain; if it follows the naming
patterns of countless other peoples, it probably translates to
something like "those people over there." In the manner of many
other nations, the Chemehuevi call themselves Núwu, "the
people."

CHEOPS PYRAMID

The writer and traveler George Wharton James named this 5,401-
foot butte for its fanciful resemblance to the Great Pyramid of
Cheops, one of the seven wonders of the ancient world, writing that "it has a peculiar shape as of some
quaint and Oriental device of symbolic sig-
nificance." Cheops Pyramid is the eastern-
most of the complex of features
named after Egyptian
deities, among them
Isis Temple (q.v.)
and the Tower of
Set (q.v.).

CHEYAVA FALLS

Cheyava means something like "on again, off again" in Hopi.
Emery and Ellsworth Kolb, who discovered the falls in 1908,
named this remote waterfall in Clear Creek Canyon for its

intermittent flow. The falls can be seen from points on the Tonto Trail. *Cheeava*, of uncertain etymology and meaning, is also the Paiute name for a spring near Zion National Park.

CHIAVRIA POINT

Juan Chiavria was a Maricopa leader who participated with King S. Woolsey (*see* Woolsey Point) in the Bloody Tanks massacre. Frank Bond (*see* Alsap Butte) named this point in his honor.

CHIKAPANAGI MESA

The writer George Wharton James named this low-lying mesa after a young Havasupai who guided him through the Canyon, saying that Chikapanagi (sometimes spelled Chikapangi) meant "bat," and that the unfortunate man resembled one.

CHUAR BUTTE

According to Canyon explorer Frederick Dellenbaugh, 6,394-foot Chuar Butte and nearby Chuar Creek owe their names to "one of Powell's Kaibab Indians, 'Chuar-oo-um-peak,' young Kaibab chief, usually called Frank by settlers and Chuar by his own people." Jacob Hamblin, the Mormon pioneer, arranged for Chuar to guide Powell through the eastern Canyon, and Chuar also accompanied Powell to the Hopi Mesas.

On June 30, 1956, which the almanacs show as a "reasonably clear day," two airplanes flying on parallel courses from Los Angeles somehow crossed paths and crashed over Chuar Butte, killing all 128 people aboard. Pieces of the wreckage were scattered all over the butte. Most are now gone, having long since been removed, but occasionally travelers will turn up a fragment of metal that commemorates that sad event, the gravest of the many air disasters the Canyon has witnessed.

CLEMENT POWELL BUTTE

Walter Clement Powell, a cousin of John Wesley Powell (*see* Powell Plateau), participated in the latter's second Canyon expedition as the assistant to photographer William O. Beaman. Walter posted letters and photographs to the *Chicago Tribune* that excited considerable public interest in his cousin's scientific work.

COCHISE BUTTE

Cochise (ca. 1805–1874) was a famed war leader of the Chiricahua Apaches. In 1861 he was unfairly accused of stealing cattle and an adopted Apache boy from a ranch in the Sonoita Valley of southern Arizona. Protesting his innocence, he fled from the soldiers who had arrested him and was wounded in the escape. This set off a chain of confrontations, with Apaches killing Anglos and Anglos killing Apaches, that lasted for more than ten years until peace was made. Cochise, much admired by even his staunchest opponents, died of cancer in 1874 and was buried in the Dragoon Mountains of southeastern Arizona. "After burial," wrote Indian agent Thomas W. Jeffords (*see* Jeffords Point), "the Apaches rode their ponies back and forth over the area about the grave, completely obliterating it."

COCONINO PLATEAU

The people called the Coconino Indians by Spanish and early Anglo-American explorers were Havasupai; the term *Coconino*, the meaning of which is unclear, is Hopi. The famed biologist C. Hart Merriam named this high, broad plain in 1892.

COCOPAH POINT

The Cocopah Indians live near the confluence of the Colorado River and the Gulf of California. The name is believed to mean "those who live beside the river."

COGSWELL BUTTE

This low rise above Surprise Valley is named for Raymond A. Cogswell (1873–1964), who accompanied Julius F. Stone (*see* Stone Creek) as photographer on Stone's 1909 expedition.

COLORADO RIVER

Rising from sources in the Colorado Rockies and, indirectly,
the Wind River Mountains of
Wyoming, the Colorado flows
1,450 miles to its confluence
with the Gulf of California.
The name means "reddish" in
Spanish. Hernando Alarcón
(see Alarcón Terrace), who
mapped the confluence, called it
the Río de Buena Guía, "river of good
guidance"; Melchior Diaz called it Río del
Tisón, "firebrand river"; Juan de Oñate called it Río Grande de
Buena Esperanza, "great river of good hope"; and Hernando
Escalante (see Escalante Creek) called it Rio de Cosninos, "river
of the Coconino [Havasupai] Indians." John Wesley Powell (see
Powell Plateau) called the lower river, after the junction of the
Grand and Green Rivers, the Colorado River of the West, and
the shortened version has obtained since his time.

COLTER BUTTE

James G. H. Colter (1844–1922), an emigrant from Nova Scotia,
came to Arizona in 1872. He settled first in the high country near
Nutrioso, where he unsuccessfully farmed (although it was he
who brought the first mechanical reaper to Arizona), then relo-
cated to a ranch near Prescott, where he served as a Yavapai
County deputy sheriff. He later worked as a cattleman in New
Mexico and Kansas before returning to Prescott in the 1890s.
James Colter's son Frederick was an important figure in the complex negotiations on Colorado River water rights that eventually
led to the establishment of the Central Arizona Project.

COMANCHE POINT

George Wharton James, an English-born writer who traveled the
West extensively, named this Bissel Point after an officer of

the Atchison, Topeka & Santa Fe Railroad. Unaccountably, the United States Geographical Board later renamed it Comanche Point after the Texas Indian nation, whose territory lies far from the Colorado Plateau.

CONFUCIUS TEMPLE

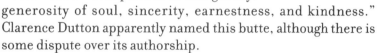

Confucius (Kung Fu Tse) was a Chinese philosopher and teacher who lived from about 551 to 479 B.C. His teachings on morality and politics are gathered in the *Analects*, a collection of dialogues and aphorisms. One saying that characterizes his thought is this: "To be able to practice five things everywhere under heaven constitutes perfect virtue: gravity, generosity of soul, sincerity, earnestness, and kindness." Clarence Dutton apparently named this butte, although there is some dispute over its authorship.

CONQUISTADOR AISLE

Also known as Aisle of the Conquistadors, this dark chasm was named, as Michael Ghiglieri remarks in his book *Canyon*, for reasons that are strictly romantic, inasmuch as no Spanish conquistador is known to have visited this section of river. The figurative conquistadors in question may instead be the American military officers who explored the lower Colorado River, among them Lieutenants Edward F. Beale and Joseph C. Ives and Captain George M. Wheeler. Government maps show the designation Conquistador Aisle after 1903, although the exact origins of the name are not known.

COPE BUTTE

This dramatic promontory takes its name from Edward D. Cope (1840–1897), who conducted paleontological studies in the Canyon in the 1870s.

CORONADO BUTTE

In 1539, Francisco Vásquez de Coronado (1510–1554), the Spanish governor of the province of Nueva Galicia, dispatched the Moorish servant Estevánico and Friar Marcos de Niza to the northern frontier of New Spain with orders to locate a group of seven cities of gold that had been reported by the errant conquistador Alvar Núñez Cabeza de Vaca. De Niza returned with mixed reports: they had found the cities, he proclaimed, but hostile Indians had murdered Estevánico. De Niza sketched out a journey of several thousands of miles, recounting, like Cabeza de Vaca, great mountains and rivers and uncounted riches. Rodrigo de Albornoz, the royal treasurer of New Spain, summarized de Niza's report:

There are seven very populous cities with great buildings. . . . The name of one where he has been is Cíbola, the others are in the Kingdom of Marata. There is very good news of other very populous countries, of their riches and good order and manner of living, also of their edifices and other things. They have houses built of stone and lime, being of three stories, and with great quantities of turquoise embedded in the doors and windows. Of animals there are camels and elephants and cattle . . .

and a great number of sheep like those of Peru, also other animals with a single horn reaching to the ground, for which reason they must feed sideways. These are not unicorns but some other kind of creature. The people are said to go clothed to the neck, like Moors. They are known to be people of solid understanding.

On February 22, 1540, Coronado set out from his capital of Compostéla with 300 Spanish soldiers and a retinue of more than 1,000 Mexican Indian bearers. They trudged northward through Sonora, eventually crossing rough mountain country that left his men and animals exhausted. From there they entered a high plateau and found a dusty mesa-top village called Shiwona, or Zuni (*see* Zuni Point), a word Spanish ears heard as Cíbola.

It was not made of gold. It was instead, Coronado reported, "a small rocky pueblo, all crumpled up, there being many farm settlements in New Spain that look better from afar." The inhabitants, whom Coronado had to battle into surrendering on July 7, 1540, seemed to have had no knowledge of precious metals. Infuriated, Coronado wrote to the regent of Mexico, Viceroy Mendoza, that Friar de Niza "has not told the truth in a single thing he has said, for everything is the very opposite of what he related except the name of the cities." Wounded in the siege of Zuni, Coronado spent the rest of the summer resting and then moved onward to the Río Grande, where a Tigua Indian told him of a great city far to the east called Quivira. Still bent on chasing down the chimera, Coronado determined that this must be Cíbola, and for the next two years he and his force trod the Great Plains as far as eastern Kansas. The Indian settlements he found were, like Zuni, innocent of gold. After taking a bad fall from his horse, Coronado turned his men—now a mere handful, thanks to war and the rigors of the trek—southwestward and plodded back to Mexico. A contemporary, Lorenzo de Tejada, wrote to the Spanish emperor: "Francisco Vásquez came to his home, and he is more able to be governed in it than to govern outside it. He is lacking in many of his former fine qualities and he is not the same man he was when your Majesty appointed him to governorship." He retained his post as governor of Nueva Galicia for only another two years. His health steadily declined, and Francisco Vásquez de Coronado died on his ranch outside Mexico City on September 22, 1554, at the age of forty-four.

CRAZY JUG POINT
A curiously shaped sandstone rock, which doubtless thirsty early prospectors called "the crazy jug," stands at the head of this North Rim point, with the Canyon below it.

CREMATION CREEK
The "event" names given this creek and its associated canyon, which lie below Lyell Butte, commemorate the discovery of an

ancient ash pit that explorer Emery Kolb believed, probably erroneously, to contain human remains.

CRYSTAL CREEK

A descriptive name "having commendatory value," as George Stewart remarks in *American Place-Names*, praises this stream's clear water. The authorship is uncertain.

DANA BUTTE

This 5,031-foot "bold headland directly north of Powell Memorial," as writer-historian Will Croft Barnes calls it, honors James Wright Dana (1813–1895), the famed American geologist. The butte is composed mostly of Redwall Limestone, and lies immediately below Hopi Point (*q.v.*). In 1919, one entrepreneur proposed connecting Hopi Point, Dana Butte, the Tower of Set (*q.v.*), and Tiyo Point (*q.v.*) with an aerial tramway, a technically feasible plan that fortunately has never been realized.

DARWIN PLATEAU

On graduating from Cambridge University, Charles Darwin (1809–1882) signed on to participate in the five-year scientific cruise of *H.M.S. Beagle*. In those crowded quarters, Darwin had room only for a few personal items. Among them were the three volumes of Charles Lyell's *Principles of Geology*, one of the key texts of nineteenth-century science (*see* Lyell Plateau). From Lyell and other writers Darwin had accepted the theory of uniformitarianism; the observations he made on the circumglobal voyage of the *Beagle* led to his adaptation of that theory to form the idea of natural selection, by which species of plants and animals develop through variations that increase those species' chances of survival and reproducibility. Darwin never laid eyes on the Colorado River, but many spots along its course lend support to his observation, in his 1859 book *The Origin of Species*, that "it is interesting to contemplate an entangled bank, clothed with many plants of many kinds, with birds singing on the bushes, with various insects flitting about, and with worms crawling through the damp earth, and to reflect that these elaborately constructed forms, so different from each other, and dependent on each other in so complex a manner, have all been produced by laws acting around us." The scientists who worked in Grand Canyon, most of them heavily influenced by Darwin, have found in the geological record it contains plenty of evidence of those laws, and they honored Darwin by according him a place in the Canyon's roster.

DEAD HORSE MESA
The origins of this clearly commemorative name for a bluff above Mile 150 are not known, but it has appeared so on the map since the early 1900s.

DEMARAY POINT
This elevation just below Zoroaster Canyon is named for Arthur E. Demaray (1887–1958), director of the National Park Service in the early 1950s.

DE MOTTE PARK
Alternately called V. T. Park after a nearby ranch, this large natural meadow on the northern border of Grand Canyon National Park's North Rim is now the site of the Canyoneers, Inc., Alpine Lodge. John Wesley Powell (*see* Powell Plateau) named it in honor of Harry C. De Motte, a member of his 1872 expedition who left the party at Lees Ferry (*q.v.*) for reasons that are obscure.

After gaining statehood in 1896, Utah made a number of legislative attempts to annex the Arizona Strip, the little-populated portion of the present state that lies north of the Colorado River. Pioneer writer Sharlot Hall (1870–1943), then the territorial historian by gubernatorial appointment after having served as an editor of Charles Lummis's magazine *Out West*, set out by buckboard to explore the Strip in 1911. She did so both to satisfy her curiosity—it was a part of Arizona she had not seen, as indeed few Arizonans had—and to arm the territorial government with information to fend off Utah's bid to incorporate the largely Mormon area. In her report she wrote,

We were going back through "V. T." Park where the V. T. Cattle Company located its headquarters ranch in the early days of the cattle business in the Buckskin country, and where there is now a forest ranger's station as well as the ranch buildings.

The fall rodeo was going on and a lot of stock cattle were being driven out for shipment to other ranges, for the country here, once over-stocked unmercifully in the day of the open range, is being built up to splendid condition by the care of the Forest Service in limiting grazing to what the range will really support.

Some day there will be hundreds of little homes all through these narrow, park-valleys down which our road winds. Just now we are stopped for dinner where the road turns off to the Jacob's Lake sawmill and there are two pretty little places just below us, comfortable log cabins with fields and pasture under "worm fence" or split rails, or pine logs rolled into line. Oats and rye and probably barley would grow anywhere here and as fine potatoes and hardy vegetables as one could wish. The snow is too heavy to stay up all winter but it is only two days' drive down to Fredonia with its good school and pleasant village settlement for winter.

It began to rain as we broke camp after dinner and I walked far ahead of the wagon to gather agates. This stretch of road toward Jacob's Lake has more beautiful agates than any place I have seen in Arizona; they glistened in the rain and I picked up all I could carry and then sorted them out and reluctantly threw away all but the finest. Many of them would cut beautifully and the color and grain are very fine. No doubt they would have some commercial value if gathered carefully.

Those hundreds of little homes have failed to materialize, but rockhounds still flock to De Motte Park and its environs in search of the agates Hall celebrated.

DESERT VIEW POINT

A classically descriptive name, to the point of being prosaic, honoring the point's sweeping view of the Painted Desert.

DEUBENDORFF RAPID

S. S. Deubendorff (spelled Dubendorff in some sources and on some maps), was a boatman on Julius Stone and Nathan Galloway's 1909 Colorado River expedition, and his contributions are honored by this place name at Mile 132. In *Canyon Country*, Julius Stone writes that Deubendorff overturned a boat on the last rapid in Conquistador Aisle (*q.v.*): "His head is pretty badly cut and with the blood streaming over his face he surely looks unhandsome. Still, his first words are, 'I'd sure like to try that again. I *know* I can run it!'" He showed similar sangfroid throughout the trip.

DEVA TEMPLE

Surveyor Clarence Dutton named this 7,339-foot bluff after an aspect of Durga, in Hindu mythology the wife of Shiva (*see* Shiva Temple).

DE VACA TERRACE

Early in March of 1536 four wraithlike figures, dressed in tattered animal skins, stole out upon the coastal plain of Sonora, making their way seaward. On the outskirts of a small ranch they were hailed by a Spanish sentry, who demanded to know their identity. The leader spoke, and gladly. "Having almost despaired of finding Christians again," he recalled, "we could hardly restrain our excitement."

On April 1st the four were led to the provincial capital of Culiacán, where their leader told a fantastic story. His name, he related, was Alvar Núñez Cabeza de Vaca, the forty-four-year-old scion of landed gentry. His noble companions were Andres

Dorantes de Carranza and Alonso de Castillo Maldonado, accompanied by Dorantes's Moorish servant, a manumitted slave called Estevánico. For more than two years they had been wandering on foot from the coast of Texas, where they had been shipwrecked with the ill-fated Narváez expedition in the winter of 1528. For six years they had remained on an island they had named Malhado, Bad Luck, to commemorate the event, trading with the Karankawa Indians and passing the time as best they could. Finally, despairing of ever being rescued, their numbers thinned from some 300 by disease, hunger, and Indian attacks to these remaining four, they waded to the mainland and set out on an overland journey far outside the compass of Spanish geography.

They saw and did miraculous things, Cabeza de Vaca reported. He himself had raised Indians, Lazarus-like, from the grave, had cured blindness and relieved illness, had preached the gospel of Jesus to countless nations, who honored him and his companions as gods. To be sure, they had had their share of hardships, crossing sun-blasted deserts for days without hope of finding water, enduring meals of mush made from tallgrass and ground seeds, losing their youth to the rigors of aimless travel. They reported passing through towering mountains and rolling grasslands, fording swollen rivers and traversing the territories of Indians friendly and hostile. One amicable band, who may have been Akimel O'odham, gave him, he said, "innumerable deerhide and cotton blankets, the latter better than those of New Spain, beads made of coral from the South Sea, fine turquoises from the north—in fact, everything they had, including a fine gift to me of five emerald arrowheads such as they use in their singing and dancing." Six hundred Indian acolytes had followed them, he continued, almost to the point where they first encountered other Spaniards.

One story above all captured the attention of his audience. The Indians to their north, de Vaca averred, had pointed the direction toward seven fabulous adjoining cities made entirely of gold. Their name, he said, was Cíbola (see Coronado Butte).

As his story spread, Cabeza de Vaca was accused of sorcery and cannibalism and was deported to Spain. Not long after his arrival there he published a memoir called *Naufragios* (Shipwrecks), full of still more fantastic adventures. Appreciative readers in the court rewarded his alleged exploits with an appointment as the royal captain-general of the Province of La Plata, comprising modern northern Argentina, Uruguay, and southern Paraguay. There he accumulated riches until he was deposed in 1544, exiled to Algeria, and finally allowed to return to Spain. He died nearly penniless in Seville in 1557.

DIAMOND CANYON

Lying outside the national park, Diamond Canyon, once locally famous for its population of feral burros, enters the Colorado below 3,512-foot Diamond Peak at Mile 225. Lieutenant Joseph Ives named it without explanation in 1857, although Arizona historian Will Croft Barnes notes that an effort was made to revive a diamond mine swindle here in the 1880s that had earlier been perpetrated in Utah and Colorado. In the scam, investors were persuaded to put money into diamond mines on the Colorado Plateau that would put the mines of South Africa to shame. A. F. Banta (*see* Banta Point) exposed this fraud, but not before dozens of investors had been bilked.

Ives's illustrator Heinrich Balduin Möllhausen recorded his impressions of Diamond Canyon in his journal:

> *The steep walls offered a strange play of colors. The first eight hundred feet were predominantly dark-brown and blue-black, while the upper strata glowed in a most beautiful rose, yellow, blue, or green, depending upon how the setting sun picturesquely illuminated these formations, which had been deposited upon the other across the ages. The unusual clarity of the air made distant objects appear much closer than they actually were.*

After traveling throughout the Southwest, Möllhausen returned to his native Germany and wrote a series of Western romances that first brought the Colorado Plateau to the attention of Europeans.

In 1872 Frederick Dellenbaugh named a rise on the Uinkaret Plateau, across the river, after the gem. "When I sighted to [it]," he writes in *A Canyon Voyage*, "for want of a better name, I recorded it temporarily as Diamond Butte, remembering the crystals, and the name became fixed, which shows how unintentionally names are sometimes bestowed."

DIANA TEMPLE

The name of this 6,400-foot butte honors Diana, the Roman goddess of the hunt, analog of the Greek goddess Artemis. She was a protector of bears and wolves, which abounded in historic times in the region of Grand Canyon.

DIRTY DEVIL RIVER

The Dirty Devil, which empties into Lake Powell just above Glen Canyon outside the national park, once carried the more dignified name Frémont. John Wesley Powell hoped thereby to honor his fellow soldier-explorer John Charles Frémont (1813–1890), who later served as territorial governor of Arizona. However, local usage confined Frémont's name to the principal upper fork of the river above Hanksville, Utah. Frémont explored the region only incidentally.

The story has it that when Jack Sumner (*see* Sumner Butte), one of Powell's boatmen, first negotiated the roiling waters of the confluence he yelled, "Watch it, men, she's a dirty devil!" Ellsworth Kolb offers a different interpretation in his book *Through the Grand Canyon from Wyoming to Mexico:* "The Dirty Devil was muddy and alkaline, while warm springs containing sulfur and other minerals added to its unpalatable taste. After tasting it we could well understand the feeling of Jack Sumner, whose remark, after a similar trial, suggested its name to Major Powell." (*See* Bright Angel Creek.)

DOX CASTLE

The name of this pillar and the associated Dox Formation honors "Miss Virginia Dox, pioneer lady visitor to the interior of the Canyon at this point." This according to the writer George Wharton James, who did not elaborate on why Miss Dox should have merited the recognition. In fact, she explored many buttes in the Canyon and gave Holy Grail Temple (*q.v.*) its original name, Bass Tomb.

THE DRAGON

This fancifully named island plateau lies close enough to the complex of features named after Arthurian legend to suspect that it commemorates one of the many dragons Arthur slew, although in point of fact the origins are unclear. Stephen J. Pyne writes in *Fire on the Rim*,

> At one time, The Dragon was a narrow peninsula, flanked on both sides by ancient faults that have allowed the Canyon to penetrate deeply into the [Kaibab] Plateau. The thinness of the residual peninsula has encouraged its erosion into an uncanny approximation of a sleeping dragon. . . . From the gorge of Crystal Creek to the mesas of body and head, The Dragon is higher than any peak east of the Rockies. Its colossal bulk gives it a sphinx-like quality. But in a Canyon packed with gargantuan rock masses, the eccentricities of The Dragon are lost amid an overabundance of geologic and scenic exotica.

DRUMMOND PLATEAU

This area is named for Willis Drummond, who assisted John Wesley Powell in the preparation of his famous 1878 *Report on the Lands of the Arid Region of the United States*.

DUNN BUTTE

Along with the Howland brothers, William H. Dunn left the first Powell expedition (*see* Separation Rapid) of 1869 after a dispute with its leader. The three were murdered—whether by Mormons or Paiutes is a matter of debate among historians—an event that seems not to have moved Powell much. Frank Bond (*see* Alsap Butte) named this butte in Dunn's honor.

The name of Dunn Butte illustrates the nineteenth-century explorer George Ruxton's remark that in his time

Western geographical features were "invariably christened after some unfortunate [traveler], killed there in an Indian fight, or treacherously slaughtered by lurking savages." (*See*, however, Woolsey Point for the other side of that coin.)

DUPPA BUTTE

On a winter's day in 1868, the story goes, an Englishman named Darrell Duppa, an early booster of the Salt River Valley whose imagination was fueled by a classical education and a diet of whisky, drunkenly clambered atop a knoll near Hayden's Mill, in what is now Tempe, and declared that he and his fellows would emulate their Hohokam predecessors in the region by building a great metropolis of canals and gardens. Likening their efforts to the deathless bird of Greek mythology, Duppa proclaimed, "A new city will spring phoenix-like upon the ruins of a former civilization."

The name Phoenix stuck, and was made official later that spring, when territorial legislators applied it to the newly established electoral precinct. For his service, Frank Bond (*see* Alsap Butte) named this Grand Canyon locale in Duppa's honor.

DUTTON POINT

Clarence E. Dutton, the famed surveyor, is responsible for many names in the Grand Canyon (*see*, for example, Vishnu Point), but we owe this name to George Wharton James, who wrote, "Dutton point I named for the distinguished geologist, poet and brilliant writer, Major C. E. Dutton."

In *Beyond the Hundredth Meridian*, Wallace Stegner honors Dutton further: "Dutton is almost as much the genius loci of the Grand Canyon as Muir is of Yosemite. And though it is Powell's monument to which tourists walk after dinner to watch the sunset from the South Rim, it is with Dutton's eyes, as often as not, that they see."

Dutton himself wrote of the Grand Canyon's features, "If any of these stupendous creations had been planted upon the plains of central Europe it would have influenced modern art as profoundly as Fujiyama has influenced the decorative art of Japan." Elsewhere in his famed book *Tertiary History of the Grand Canyon*, Dutton subtly defended his own poetic tendencies when naming features of the Canyon (*see* Point Sublime): "Give the imagination an inch and it is apt to take an ell, and the fundamental requirement of scientific method—accuracy of statement—is imperiled. But in the Grand Canyon district there is no such danger. The stimulants which are demoralizing elsewhere are necessary here to exalt the mind sufficiently to comprehend the sublimity of the subjects."

EHRENBERG POINT

Hermann Ehrenberg (1816–1866) was a German mining engineer who had seen much adventure in his day, having fought in the Texas War of Independence and written of it for the European press. He returned to the United States in the early 1840s and traveled by the Oregon Trail to the Pacific, where he proceeded on to Hawaii and Polynesia. Eventually he came to the Southwest, where he mapped the newly acquired territory of the Gadsden Purchase and undertook several mining ventures. He was murdered at the stagecoach station outside of present-day Mecca, California, while carrying gold to San Diego; his killer was never identified. A small town on the southern Colorado River bears his name, as does this headland, awarded the designation by decision of the United States Geographical Board.

ELAINE CASTLE

Surveyor Richard T. Evans, who in 1902 bestowed most of the Arthurian names that points in the Canyon bear, named Elaine Castle after Elaine of Astolat, Lancelot's lover.

ELVES CHASM

Inarguably one of the finest poetic names in the Canyon, Elves Chasm, at Mile 116.5, was so called for the strange, many-hued travertine formations within it and the fanciful notion that elves must mine them. The chasm is also nearly tropical, and seemingly out of place, in its abundance of ferns and orchids. John Wesley Powell (see Powell Plateau) wrote of the area, "The elements that unite to make the Grand Canyon the most sublime spectacle in nature are multifarious and exceedingly diverse. . . . Besides the elements of form, there are elements of color, for here the colors of the heavens are rivaled by the colors of the rocks. The rainbow is not more replete with hues."

EMMA, MOUNT

Clarence Dutton (see Dutton Point) named pineclad Mount Emma, on the Uinkaret Plateau, for John Wesley Powell's wife Emma in 1882. One of the boats used on Powell's second Canyon expedition was named the *Emma Dean*. Quite by coincidence, one of John D. Lee's wives (see Lees Ferry), whom Powell met, was also named Emma.

ENFILADE POINT

Enfilade is a military term for a position that introduces crossfire into a field of fire, suggesting that the unknown author of this place name for a promontory above Mile 124 had experience in warfare.

ESCALANTE CREEK

Francisco Silvestre Vélez de Escalante (1750–1780) was a Spanish-born Franciscan missionary. In 1774 he was assigned to a parish in New Mexico, from which he traveled the next year to visit the Hopi Mesas. In June 1776 Francisco Atanasio Domínguez, an ecclesiastical superior, asked Escalante to accompany him on an expedition to chart a land route from Santa Fe, New Mexico, to Monterey, on the California coast. With seven others, they left Santa Fe on July 29, 1776. By late September, they reached the Green River in northern Utah, and then turned west to a point near the Great Salt Lake. In mid-October, having traveled south, they crossed onto the Kaibab Plateau (*q.v.*) and eventually forded the Colorado River at a point northeast of the present Grand Canyon National Park, the famed "Crossing of the Fathers." Escalante spent the next few years in Santa Fe writing an account of their 1,700-mile journey and preparing a history of New Mexico. Escalante died while traveling to Mexico City for treatment of an unspecified ailment. He was only thirty years old.

Almon H. Thompson (*see* Thompson Point) suggested this name, as he did that of Escalante, Utah, which earlier bore the uninspiring name Spud Valley.

ESPEJO BUTTE

The Spanish conquistador Antonio de Espejo (ca. 1531–ca. 1587) came to America as an agent of the Inquisition, but he became something of a freebooter and all-around rascal with no visible means of support. In 1583, he organized an exploring party from Santa Barbara, New Mexico, and ventured into what is now Arizona, visiting the Hopi Mesas and, guided by Hopis, traveling as far west as present-day Jerome, where they discovered mineral and copper outcrops that would be mined three centuries later. Espejo wrote a self-aggrandizing report on his travels that inspired Juan de Oñate to lead a colonizing party into New Mexico fifteen years after Espejo returned to Mexico City. Why Espejo should have been honored by a name in the Grand Canyon is not clear.

THE ESPLANADE

Canyon surveyor Clarence Dutton dubbed this seemingly smooth rock platform of the Supai Formation The Esplanade in 1882, likening it to a public walkway of the same name in New

York's Central Park. On closer inspection, Colin Fletcher discovered, as he writes in *The Man Who Walked Through Time*, that

> *the apparently flat Esplanade imposed a consistently serpentine route. Every step was zig or zag: zig along a sidecanyon; zig again for a side-sidecanyon; then zag along its far side for a new side-sidecanyon; and then another zig up a side-side-sidecanyon. And the going was almost never level. All day long I kept having to cross or to detour laboriously around little tributary gullies that were hardly deeper than suburban living rooms.*

EVANS BUTTE

The Welsh cartographer Richard T. Evans, author of many names in Grand Canyon, secures his immortality in the name of this bluff at the end of Sagittarius Ridge.

EVOLUTION AMPHITHEATER

See Huxley Terrace.

EXCALIBUR

The name of this serrated rise, lying near other features bearing Arthurian names, honors the sword given to King Arthur by the Lady of the Lake.

FAN ISLAND

This small butte in Hakatai Canyon is descriptively named; its top was thought to resemble an unfolded hand fan.

FARVIEW POINT

Farview Point, on the East Rim, affords a vista of the Painted Desert, whence its descriptive name.

FERN GLEN

This shaded canyon at Mile 168 boasts a perennial spring that feeds an abundance of maidenhair ferns.

FISKE BUTTE

This rise bears the name of John Fiske (1842–1901), an early American proponent of evolutionary theory.

FORSTER CANYON

William Forster (1871–1925) helped map the Supai Quadrangle for the United States Geological Survey. He was one of the first Anglos to see Elves Chasm (*q.v.*) as well. This low canyon lies opposite Alarcón Terrace.

FOSSIL CANYON

The United States Geological Survey named Fossil Canyon and nearby Fossil Bay and Fossil Rapids (at Mile 125) descriptively in 1927 for the many fossils found there. In his journal, explorer John Wesley Powell takes note of a number of Havasupai farms near the canyon's opening at the Colorado River.

FREYA CASTLE

Lying below Cape Royal on Walhalla Plateau (*q.v.*), this bluff is happily named inasmuch as Freya, the Norse goddess, transported the dead killed in Wotan's service (*see* Wotans Throne, which lies nearby) to the afterlife, or Valhalla.

GALAHAD POINT

Galahad, the purest of heart of all the knights of the Round Table, was the son of Lancelot and Elaine. After Arthur's death, it fell to him to retrieve the Holy Grail. Like so many Arthurian names in the Canyon, that of Galahad Point was suggested by the cartographer Richard T. Evans in 1902.

GALLOWAY CANYON

Nathan Galloway—whose family name comes from the Scots Gaelic for "place of the enemy Gaels"—was a trapper in the Grand Canyon who hired on to a number of boating parties down the Grand Canyon, including that of William Richmond in 1897 and that of Julius F. Stone in 1909.

GARCÉS TERRACE

Francisco Garcés (1738–1781), a missionary-soldier, explored much of what is now western and northern Arizona, providing the most accurate geographical survey of the time. He was also the first European to descend into Havasu Canyon. Garcés was later rewarded with a curate at the confluence of the Gila and Colorado Rivers among the Quechan, or Yuma, Indians. There he introduced Spanish-style agriculture, including the cultivation of wheat that he brought from Mexico (and that soon was "so well sprouted that the best irrigated wheat in our country does not equal it"), black-eyed peas, watermelons, and muskmelons, all for export to settlements on the Gulf of California. Closest to Garcés's heart was black mustard, the seed Jesus likened to the kingdom of heaven, which the Quechan grew in commercial quantities and sold throughout Mexico and California. Alas for Garcés, his was not to be the Garden of Eden. A group of Quechans, rebelling against Spanish rule, clubbed him to death as he said mass. The provincial governor of New Spain sent a punitive expedition the next year to avenge Garcés's death, and Spanish soldiers killed some 200 Indians and took a like number as slaves.

GARDEN CREEK

This small stream below the South Rim provided water for Indian Gardens (*q.v.*).

GATAGAMA POINT

The United States Geological Survey named this point and its associated terrace in 1925 for a Havasupai family who lived nearby.

GAWAIN ABYSS

Gawain was a knight of the Round Table who, in Arthurian legend, fought the Green Knight, the devil in disguise. Cartographer Richard T. Evans named this canyon below Shinumo Amphitheater in 1902.

GEIKIE PEAK

Sir Archibald Geikie (1835–1924), director general of the Geological Survey of the United Kingdom, studied volcanism in the Grand Canyon and wrote several reports on that process. This peak was named in his honor in 1908.

GRAND SCENIC DIVIDE

William W. Bass (*see* Bass Camp) named this geographical point descriptively. It marks the division between the Tonto Platform and upper Granite Gorge to the east.

GRANDVIEW POINT

John Hance named this point and its associated trail, which Peter Berry constructed, in 1892. The trail is no longer maintained. Berry, a miner who took copper from Horseshoe Mesa below, later managed the Grand View Hotel at this site.

GRANITE GORGE

The famed Canyon explorer John Wesley Powell named this long eastern canyon in his journal of August 14, 1869, writing, "We can see but a little way into the granite gorge, and it looks threatening."

GRAPEVINE CANYON

The origins of this name, which has been current since 1901, are unclear. Some writers suggest that the heaped boulders at the mouth of the canyon reminded early boatmen of grapes on a vine, whereas others believe that a stand of wild grapes somewhere along the Tonto Trail gave the canyon its name. This seems the likelier choice.

GREAT THUMB MESA

Frank Bond (*see* Alsap Butte) suggested this descriptive name in 1932 after viewing this large plateau from the air, remarking that it looked like an extended thumb.

GREAT UNCONFORMITY

John Wesley Powell (*see* Powell Plateau) named the Great Unconformity in 1876 to describe huge lacunae in the geological record of the Grand Canyon. In geological terms, an unconformity is a discontinuity in stratification: an old layer of rock is overlain by a younger one without the expected depositions representing the intervening years, usually because those depositions have been eroded away. In the case of the Great Unconformity, Zoroaster Granite cuts through 1.7-billion-year-old Vishnu Schist, both ending at a layer of conglomerate overlain by Tapeats Sandstone. Their boundary marks a missing 250 million years in the geological record, and it is accounted for by a massive erosion of Precambrian rock about 545 million years ago. That rock, by most estimates, was about 13,000 feet thick at one time.

John Burroughs, the great naturalist, described its appearance in a 1910 article for *Century* magazine:

> *How distinctly it looked like a new day in creation where the horizontal, yellowish-gray beds of the Cambrian were laid down upon the dark, amorphous, and twisted older granite! How carefully the level strata had been fitted to the shapeless mass beneath it! It all looked like the work of a master mason; apparently you could put the point of your knife where one formation ended and the other began. The older rock suggested chaos and turmoil, the other suggested order and plan, as if the builder had said, "Now upon this foundation we will build our house."*

GREENLAND SPRING

Mormon ranchers in the Canyon named this water source, which lies on Walhalla Plateau (*q.v.*), once called the Greenland Plateau. Some early maps show the spring as Greenland Glades.

GUINEVERE CASTLE
Cartographer Richard T. Evans named this 7,257-foot butte after King Arthur's wife, whose affair with Lancelot forms a major turn in the Arthurian legendary cycle.

GUNTHER CASTLE
In Germanic mythology, Gunther is the king on whose orders the hero Siegfried (see Siegfried Pyre) was slain. It is not at all clear why the name of this decidedly minor figure in world religion should have been applied to this 7,189-foot butte west of the Kwagunt Valley.

HAKATAI CANYON
Hakatai is an English transliteration of the Hualapai word for the Colorado River, coming from a phrase that means "backbone of the river." William W. Bass (see Bass Camp) operated an asbestos mine here in the early 1900s. As of this writing, the canyon is closed to the public.

HALL BUTTE
Andrew Hall was a young boatman on John Wesley Powell's 1869 Canyon expedition. A native of Scotland, Hall evidently had a gift for tall tales; in his journal, Powell notes that he was not bound "by unnecessary scruples in giving to his narratives those embellishments which help to make a story complete." (Powell's remark anticipates another by Canyon habitué Edward Abbey: "Never let the facts get in the way of a good story.") Frank Bond (see Alsap Butte) named the 5,530-foot butte in Hall's honor in 1932.

HANCE CREEK
John Hance (1813–1919) came to Arizona Territory shortly after the end of the Civil War, in which, he said, he had served as a Confederate—or, depending on his audience, a Union—cavalry officer. He settled in 1883 at the South Rim of the Grand Canyon. He maintained he was the first Anglo to do so, a fact he made much of when other settlers entered his once-private domain.

Although his interest was in finding riches in the form of minerals—the inactive Hance Asbestos Mine bears his name—Hance recognized that the area held the promise of being a premier tourist destination in the opening West. He accordingly built a small lodge at Glendale Springs and, in 1884, began to widen an ancient trail, the Grand Canyon's first recreational walking path. As Buckey O'Neill (see O'Neill Butte) once remarked, "God made the cañon, John Hance the trails. Without the other, neither would be complete."

Hance was renowned for his hospitality. When not serving as impromptu forest ranger, postmaster, and trail guide, he regaled his guests with improbably tall tales that earned him a place in the annals of Arizona folklore, along with the sobriquet "the Münchhausen of the West." He claimed to have dug out the Grand Canyon himself in his search for precious metals, for instance, and said that the San Francisco Peaks were just piled-up fill dirt. He spun a wonderful account of how he and his favorite horse descended into the Canyon on the backs of passing clouds. And he astonished credulous listeners by describing how he often entertained himself by jumping from spire to spire in the inner gorge.

His tales were not always met with admiration. W. W. Hawkins, a longtime resident of the Canyon region, recalled,

I knew Hance long before he had dreamed the Canyon would help make him famous; I ate venison stew with him when he was but a cowboy in the employ of the proprietor of the Hull ranch: I wrote the first account of those peculiar and exaggerated yarns of his that gained him his fame as the "Münchhausen of the West." It was on these yarns alone that his fame reposed. He was never a guide. He knew nothing of the Canyon, east or west, twenty miles from the trail that unfortunately was named after him. He never read a line of its history, and never cared to know who first discovered it. He got lost years after the Canyon was being visited by great numbers of whites, when he attempted to guide a party to the home of the Havasupai Indians, whose ancestors made the trail which he discovered and claimed on his own.

Hance Rapid, a jumble of redwall boulders at Mile 76.5, bears the storyteller's name. So, too, does the old Hance Trail, a precipitous, washed-out route along Hance Canyon into the inner gorge, which the biologist C. Hart Merriam used while mapping out his schemata of North American biological life zones. (The new Hance Trail descends elsewhere, down Red Canyon.) A visitor recorded a descent down the old trail:

> For the first two miles it is a sort of Jacob's ladder, zigzagging at an unrelenting pitch down a steep and nearly uniform decline caused by a sliding geological fault and centuries of frost and rain. At the end of two miles a comparatively gentle slope is reached, known as the First Level, some 2,500 feet below the rim; that is to say—for such figures have to be impressed objectively upon the mind—five times the height of St. Peter's, the Pyramid of Cheops, or the Strasburg Cathedral; eight times the height of the Bartholdi Statue of Liberty; eleven times the height of Bunker Hill Monument. Looking back from this level the huge picturesque towers that border the rim shrink to pigmies and seem to crown a perpendicular wall, unattainably far in the sky. Yet less than one-half the descent has been made, and less than one-third the entire distance of the trail to the river accomplished. Hance's Rock Cabin lies only a short distance ahead, where dinner and rest are to be had under the shade of cottonwoods by the side of a living spring.

The Hance Trail was free for the use of "Honest John" Hance's guests; others paid a toll. Even with that income, however, Hance died in poverty in Flagstaff, in 1919.

HANCOCK BUTTE

Frank Bond (*see* Alsap Butte) named this butte for William A. Hancock (1831–1902), who served in the Army at Fort Yuma in the mid-1860s and moved to the Salt River Valley in 1870. He surveyed the townsite for what would become

Phoenix (*see* Duppa Butte) and served as that city's first sheriff and, later, assistant U.S. district attorney.

HANSBROUGH POINT

This pillar off Marble Canyon is named after Peter Hansbrough, an unfortunate member of Robert Brewster Stanton's 1890 expedition (*see* Stanton Point) who drowned in nearby 25 Mile Rapid. "We buried him under an overhanging cliff," Stanton wrote, "and named a magnificent point opposite 'Point Hansbrough.'" Stanton also cut Hansbrough's initials into the cliff's base.

HATTAN BUTTE

Frank Bond (*see* Alsap Butte) named this butte after Andrew Hattan, the cook for John Wesley Powell's second Canyon expedition. Frederick Dellenbaugh, a member of the expedition, remarks of Hattan's apparently indifferent culinary skills, "It was Andy's first experience as a cook, although he had been a soldier in the Civil War." Not that Hattan had much to work with, as Dellenbaugh recalls:

Our food supply was composed partly of jerked beef, and as this could not be put in rubber because of the grease it became more or less damp and there developed in it a peculiar kind of worm, the largest about an inch long, with multitudinous legs. There were a great many of them and they gave the beef a queer taste. In order to clear the sacks as far as possible of these undesirable denizens I several times emptied them on wide smooth rocks, and while the worms were scrambling around I scraped up the beef without many of them, but could not get rid of all. Andy's method of cooking this beef was to make a gravy with bacon fat and scorched flour and then for a few moments stew the beef in the gravy. Ordinarily this made a very palatable dish but the peculiar flavour of the beef now detracted from it, though we were so hungry that we could eat anything without a query, and our diminishing supply of rations forbade the abandonment of the valuable beef.

HAUNTED CANYON

This canyon below the North Rim is apparently named by association with nearby Phantom Creek (*see* Phantom Ranch).

HAVASU CANYON

In the Havasupai language, *havasu* means "blue-green water" and commemorates the erstwhile appearance of stream water in Havasu Falls, one of the five waterfalls along Havasu Creek. Havasu Canyon appears in some early literature as Cataract Canyon, leading to confusion with the upstream canyon in Utah that also bears this name.

In his *Narrative of the Coronado Expedition*, Pedro de Castañeda records the Spanish exploration of the area near the canyon, inhabited for several hundred years by the Havasupai:

> *After three days Captain Melgosa and one Juan Galeras and another companion, the three lightest and most agile men, made an attempt to go down. They returned about four o'clock in the afternoon, not having succeeded in reaching the bottom. They said they had been down about a third of the way, and that the river seemed very large. Those who stayed above had guessed some huge rocks on the sides of the cliffs might be as tall as a man, but those who went down swore that when they reached those rocks they were bigger than the great tower of Seville in Spain.*

Some scholars believe that these huge rocks might have been buttes above Granite Gorge farther east.

Supai Village, the Havasupai center that lies some six miles up Havasu Canyon from the Colorado River, was badly damaged by floods in the winter of 1993.

HAWKINS BUTTE

Frank Bond (*see* Alsap Butte) named this 4,000-foot butte for
W. R. Hawkins, cook and hunter for John Wesley Powell's first
Canyon expedition.

HAYDEN, MOUNT

Frank Bond (*see* Alsap Butte) named this 8,372-foot rise near
the Walhalla Plateau after Charles Trumbull Hayden (1825–1907),
an Arizona pioneer who established a flour mill and ferry along
the Salt River at the edge of what is now Tempe.

HERMIT BASIN

Hermit Basin, Creek, Canyon, and Trail and Eremita Mesa were
all named after Louis D. Boucher (*see* Boucher Creek), popularly
called "the Hermit" by longtime residents of the Canyon.
Boucher had a home at Dripping Spring at the head of Hermit
Creek, and by all accounts was a pleasant man who simply preferred the company of the elements to that of humans.

Of Hermit Trail, the humorist Irvin S. Cobb wrote in a 1913
Saturday Evening Post article:

> The casual visitor to the Grand Cañon first of all takes the rim
> drive; then he essays Bright Angel Trail, which is sufficiently
> scary for his purposes until he gets used to it; and after that he
> grows more adventurous and tackles Hermit Trail, which is a
> marvel of corkscrew convolutions, gimleting its way down this
> red abdominal gash of a cañon to the very gizzard of the world.

HILLERS BUTTE

Frank Bond (*see* Alsap Butte) named this 5,600-foot butte after
John K. Hillers, photographer for John Wesley Powell's
second Canyon expedition.

HINDU AMPHITHEATER

Clarence Dutton (*see* Dutton Point) named this
4,072-foot depression, remarking, "The archi-
tectural details are always striking, and by their

profusion and richness suggest an Oriental character." The name is not parallel with other entries in his exotic nomenclature, which follows religious and mythological themes rather than ethnic or linguistic ones.

HOLY GRAIL TEMPLE

The Holy Grail was the chalice from which Christ drank at the Last Supper. In Christian myth, the Grail then disappeared, and much of the Arthurian cycle of legends involves the search for this sacred relic. Holy Grail Temple was originally called Bass Tomb, after William W. Bass (see Bass Camp). Virginia Dox (see Dox Castle) gave Bass Tomb its name, according to George Wharton James, who writes, "Many years ago the first white lady to descend the canyon at this point named this 'Bass Tomb,' and I see no reason to reject the name, for in sight of it Mr. Bass's most arduous labors have been spent, and here it is appropriate that he should have his immortal memorial." Bass's ashes were scattered over Holy Grail Temple in 1933.

HOPI POINT

The Board of Geographical Names named this South Rim point, once called Rowes Point after local cattleman Sanford Rowe (see Rowes Well), for the Hopi Indians of northeastern Arizona. *Hopitu*, the name by which the Hopi refer to themselves, means something like "unwarlike people."

HORSESHOE MESA

Peter Berry, a Canyon pioneer who helped build the Bright Angel Trail from 1890 to 1902, filed claims to mine the remarkably pure copper deposits on this mesa, which is descriptively named for its shape. (*See also* Grandview Point.) Scattered remnants of mining machinery can still be found along the mesa top.

HORN CREEK

Canyon resident Henry Gannett suggested that this small creek and its associated rapids be named for Tom Horn (1860–1903), an Army scout in the Geronimo campaign who later served as a Yavapai County deputy sheriff under Buckey O'Neill (*see* O'Neill Point). Hired to work as a detective for the ranching industry and charged with halting a cattle-rustling operation in Wyoming, Horn himself fell afoul of the law and was charged with murdering a teenage boy. He was hanged. Old friends in Arizona, Gannett among them, believed that Horn had been framed, and the creek was named after Horn just a few months after his death.

HORUS TEMPLE

Horus was a demigod of Egyptian mythology, the son of Isis and Osiris, for whom other "temples" in the Canyon are named. This one stands at about 5,700 feet.

HOTOUTA CANYON

George Wharton James, the English-born writer who made his home in the West, named this canyon after Tom Hotouta, the son of the Havasupai chief Navajo. (*See* Yunosi Point.)

HOUSE ROCK CREEK

Of the difficult passage down this section of river, where House Rock Creek meets the Colorado at Mile 17, explorer John Wesley Powell wrote, "The limestone of this canyon is often polished, and makes a beautiful marble. The rocks are of many colors— white, gray, pink, and purple, with saffron tints. It is with very great labor that we make progress, meeting with many obstructions, running rapids, letting down our boats with lines from rock to rock, and sometimes carrying boats and cargoes around bad places." Mormon pioneer Jacob Hamblin named House Rock Valley, in which this creek rises, for two large boulders that nested so as to form a shelter; locally this formation was called the Rock House or House Rock Hotel.

HOWLANDS BUTTE

Frank Bond (*see* Alsap Butte) named this butte for Oramel and Seneca Howland, brothers who, with William H. Dunn (*see* Dunn Butte) left the first Powell expedition at Separation Rapid (*q.v.*) and were subsequently killed.

HUALAPAI PLATEAU

This flatland west of Grand Canyon National Park is named after the Hualapai, or "pine-tree mountain people," whose reservation is there.

HUBBELL BUTTE

The historian and writer Will Croft Barnes named Hubbell Butte after Lorenzo Hubbell (1853–1930), a famous trader on the Navajo Reservation.

HUETHWALI, MOUNT

Huethwali means something like "white tower" in Havasupai, a fitting enough sobriquet for this 6,280-foot rise on the Darwin Plateau. The writer George Wharton James originally named it Mount Observation.

HUTTON BUTTE

Lying at the northeast corner of Grand Canyon National Park, this feature is named for Oscar Hutton (1830–1873), who, according to the contemporary historian Thomas E. Farish, "has the reputation of having personally killed more Indians than any other man in Arizona." Farish also notes that Hutton died after a mule kicked him in the head.

HUXLEY TERRACE

Lying, appropriately, between bluffs named for Charles Darwin and Alfred Wallace, this terrace honors Thomas Henry Huxley (1825–1895), an English cleric and philosopher whose support for their theories of evolution helped make Darwin's and Wallace's ideas acceptable. The writer George Wharton James records the earlier name Observation Plateau, which was displaced on maps in the early 1900s. The appropriately named Evolution Amphi-theater lies between Huxley Terrace and Spencer Terrace (*q.v.*).

INDIAN GARDENS

Indian Gardens (also Indian Garden), near the Bright Angel Trail at about 3,800 feet, was a large plot of cultivated land on what used to be called Angel Terrace. The writer and traveler George Wharton James is credited for giving it its name.

Writing in 1902, the naturalist John Muir observes, "By the Bright Angel trail the last fifteen hundred feet of the descent to the river has to be made afoot down the gorge of Indian Garden Creek. Most of the visitors do not like this part, and are content to stop at the end of the horse-trail and look down on the dull-brown flood [of the Colorado River] from the edge of the Indian Garden Plateau." The trail is no less precipitous in our time.

ISIS TEMPLE

The writer George Wharton James named this 7,012-foot bluff for Isis, the Egyptian nature goddess, whose wor-ship was one of the chief religions of the Roman Empire. With her brother and husband Osiris, Isis was the parent of Horus.

John Burroughs, the famed naturalist, wrote on a visit to the Canyon in 1909:

One of the smaller of the many geologic temples is called the temple of Isis. How it seems to be resisting the siege of time, throwing out its salients here and there, and meeting the onset of the foe like a military engineer! It is made up of four stories, and its height is about 2,500 feet. The finish at the top is a line of heavy wall probably one hundred feet high. The lines of many of these natural temples or fortresses are still more lengthened and attenuated, appearing like mere skeletons of their former selves. The forms that weather out of the formation above this, the Permian, appear to be more rotund, and tend more to domes and rounded hills.

IVES POINT

In 1857–58, Army lieutenant Joseph Christmas Ives (1828–1868) led an expedition that would complete the first systematic survey of the Canyon region. He approached the Canyon from the southwest, having traveled up the Colorado River to Black Canyon, below present Lake Mead, by a specially outfitted steamboat called the *Explorer*. Ives, for whom this point between Alarcón Terrace and Darwin Plateau is named, did not much like the country he mapped. "The region is, of course, altogether valueless," he wrote in his report to Congress. "It can be approached only from the south, and after entering it there is nothing to do but leave. Ours has been the first, and will doubtless be the last, party of whites to visit this profitless locality. It seems intended by nature that the Colorado River, along the greater portion of its lonely and majestic way, shall be forever unvisited and undisturbed."

JEFFORDS POINT

This 6,547-foot projection off the Walhalla Plateau is named for Tom Jeffords (1832–1914), an Army scout who was instrumental in negotiating peace with Cochise's band of Chiricahua Apaches in 1870.

JICARILLA POINT

This little-visited West Rim point, which lies above Pollux Temple, takes its name from the Jicarilla Apache tribe of New Mexico.

JOHNSON POINT

This 5,100-foot point near Bright Angel Creek was named by the United States Geographical Board for Frederick Johnson, a park ranger who drowned along with Glen Sturdevant (*see* Sturdevant Point) above Horn Creek in 1929.

JONES POINT

Frank Bond (*see* Alsap Butte) named this 5,300-foot overlook just east of Bright Angel Creek for S. V. Jones, a mathematician-surveyor on John Wesley Powell's second Canyon expedition.

JUMPUP CANYON

A prosaic descriptive: horses negotiating the narrow bed of this canyon have to jump up to the trail leading to the North Rim.

JUNO TEMPLE

In Roman mythology, Juno is the queen of the gods and the wife of the sky god Jupiter. This 6,200-foot butte lies alongside Jupiter Temple.

JUPITER TEMPLE

Jupiter's name derives from the Latin *deus-pater*, "god the father." If logic reigned in Grand Canyon names, the appellation of this 7,081-foot wooded slope above Chuar Creek east of the Walhalla Plateau and that of nearby, and lower, Juno Temple would have been reserved for points within the cluster of features below the South Rim named after figures of classical mythology.

KAIBAB PLATEAU

After the Tibetan plateau, the Colorado Plateau is the world's second highest. This 9,000-foot subplateau on the North Rim is among the Colorado Plateau's highest points. The name comes from the Paiute for "mountain lying down." Fray Francisco Atanasio Domínguez and Fray Silvestre Vélez de Escalante traversed it in 1776, and Escalante recorded in his diary,

We crossed it with plenty of difficulty and fatigue experienced by the horse herds, because it was very rocky besides having many gulches. . . . Here there is extensive valley land but of bad terrain, for what is not sand is a kind of ground having about three inches of rubble, and after that loose soil of different hues. . . .

Through this area runs the Río Colorado, from north-northeast to south-southwest, very deep inside a canyon, so that even if the land were good the river is of no help for farming near it. This afternoon we saw the embankments and cliffs of the river's box canyon which, when viewed along the western side, give the impression of a lengthy row of structures, but we figured it to be some box canyon of the many arroyos found on the plain.

Mormon pioneers called the plateau Buckskin Mountain, by which name it occasionally appears on maps today.

KANAB CANYON

John Wesley Powell (*see* Powell Plateau) named this canyon and its creek, which join the Colorado at Mile 143.6, after the Paiute word for willow, a tree abundant here. The tall canyon—Ellsworth Kolb describes it as a "narrow, gloomy gorge"—is lined with Muav Limestone formations. E. O. Beaman, who traversed the Grand Canyon in 1874, described Kanab Canyon thus:

Within twenty miles of the river the walls of the cañon gradually close in, until, in many places, they reach within fifty feet of each other. They also gain altitude, until, at the junction of the Colorado, they tower three thousand feet in air. The sun is seen only three hours during the day. Words are inadequate to describe the sensations of one entering the tomb-like vastness. The upper strata of the cliffs is composed of tinted sandstone, beautifully veined with purple. A few miles farther this changes to limestone, of a bluish gray, filled with slate-flint and chalcedony.

KANGAROO HEADLAND
A descriptive name: in outline this bluff evidently suggested to some unknown namer the appearance of a kangaroo, an animal that is emphatically not indigenous to the Canyon.

KIBBEY BUTTE
Pioneer historian Will Croft Barnes named this rise for Joseph H. Kibbey (1853–1929), territorial governor of Arizona from 1905 to 1909 and later a principal in the Salt River Valley Water Users Association, which successfully pressed for the construction of several dams in Arizona.

KING ARTHUR CASTLE
Also King Arthur's Castle. Richard T. Evans named this 7,344-foot bluff after King Arthur's legendary fortress, Camelot, which is thought to lie under Glastonbury Abbey or South Cadbury Castle, both on the border of England and Evans's ancestral Wales.

KOLB NATURAL BRIDGE
Emery Kolb lived at the Grand Canyon from 1902 until his death in 1976 at the age of ninety-five. With his brother Ellsworth, he ran the length of the Colorado River from Wyoming to the Gulf of California in 1911 and 1912, writing a popular book on the adventure. Kolb also ran a photographic studio at the head of the Bright Angel Trail, descending 4.6 miles each day to Indian Gardens (*q.v.*) to fetch the water needed to develop his film. This sandstone arch below Point Imperial was first discovered by Joe Hamblin, a packer for John Wesley Powell's second Canyon expedition, in 1871. Barry M. Goldwater, the famed Arizona politician, rediscovered it in 1953 and gave the natural bridge its present name. It is also called Kolb Bridge and Kolb Arch. Kolb Rapids, at Mile 205, also bears Emery Kolb's name.

KOMO POINT

This point on the westernmost reach of the Walhalla Plateau was named after a Paiute family who lived nearby.

KRISHNA SHRINE

The cartographer François Matthes named this 6,115-foot bluff after the Hindu deity, the dark avatar of Vishnu.

KWAGUNT VALLEY

Frederick Dellenbaugh, who accompanied John Wesley Powell on his second Canyon expedition, writes that Powell named this "lovely valley in the Grand Canyon" after a Paiute Indian who claimed it belonged to his family. Dellenbaugh remembers Kwagunt as being "very friendly and honest with the settlers."

LANCELOT POINT

Lancelot was Arthur's favorite knight and the protagonist of many key adventures in the Arthurian cycle of legends. His love for Arthur's wife Guinevere led to the collapse of Arthur's kingship. Cartographer Richard T. Evans named this point, as he did so many other Canyon features that bear Arthurian names.

LAVA CANYON

The United States Geological Survey named this narrow canyon at Mile 65 for its predominant volcanic rock.

LAVA CLIFF RAPID

Lava Cliff Rapid was named by Claude Birdseye (see Lava Falls) for a lava bench on the right bank just above this rapid, six miles below Separation Rapid; Lava Cliff Rapid now lies under water backed up by Hoover Dam, but in its time it was something to be reckoned with, and between it and Lower Disaster Falls lies some fantastically tough country. George Flavell, an early Canyon explorer, wrote,

> It is an awful place, and destitute to the extreme. In all its barren walls there is not a single bat's nest—not even they

would live in such an awful place. Language can convey only a faint idea of such a place, for the literature put before the public is so different in its description of the real canyon, it would not be recognized. . . . I don't think there is another such barren country in the world as the one we have passed through (unless it is the Sahara).

Neil B. Carmony and David H. Brown note, in their edition of Flavell's log, that he was describing the area around Bat Cave (Mile 266), the site of such a huge colony of bats that attempts were made to mine guano commercially there in the 1950s.

LAVA FALLS

On August 25, 1869, the famed Canyon explorer John Wesley Powell excitedly wrote of this rapid at Mile 179, "Great quantities of lava are seen on either side; and then we come to an abrupt cataract. Just over the fall a cinder cone, or extinct volcano, stands on the very brink of the canyon. What a conflict of water and fire there must have been here! Just imagine a river of molten rock running down into a river of melted snow. What a seething and boiling of the waters; what clouds of steam rolled into the heavens!" Less passionately, Claude Birdseye, an explorer for whom a North Rim point is named, wrote of it in 1923,

At 21 miles below Havasu Creek we passed a large lava pinnacle, which partly obstructs the channel but, curiously enough, forms no rapids. This is evidently the remains of a volcanic barrier, the rest of which has been eroded away by the action of the water. It is an unmistakable landmark, and voyagers by water should take warning of a very dangerous rapid, Lava Falls, a mile and a half below. The rapid is at the mouth of a canyon that comes in from the south, along the line of the Toroweap Fault, which here crosses the river, and is formed by great flows of basaltic lava from the volcanic outlets on the plateaus above. At one time the lava filled the lower part of the canyon, damming the river temporarily to the height of several hundred feet. Although the drop of Lava Falls is only ten feet, so many dangerous rocks here extend across the river that no one attempted to run through. . . . Proceeding downstream, we found that the invasions of lava continued here and there for about ten miles. We could glimpse the borders of the great lava masses and an occasional volcanic cone on the plateau above. We found clinging to the sides of the canyon near its bottom numerous flat-topped remnants of lava flows which had run many miles from the point of their entrance into the canyon, the farthest nearly 75 miles.

Some river runners consider Lava Falls Rapid to be the most dangerous in the Grand Canyon, but many more give that honor to Crystal Rapid.

LE CONTE PLATEAU
Geologist Joseph Le Conte participated in several early scientific surveys of the Canyon, initially serving as the assistant to cartographer Arnold Guyot.

LEES FERRY
John Doyle Lee joined the newly founded Mormon religion in 1838 in Missouri, where Joseph Smith had led his growing band of followers out of upstate New York. A zealous convert, Lee organized the Danites, a paramilitary group that waged a guerrilla war against the non-Mormon enemies they encountered during their sojourn in Nauvoo, Illinois. After Joseph Smith was assassinated, his successor Brigham Young adopted Lee and assigned him to help relocate the Mormon faithful to Deseret, or what is now Utah.

Lee farmed in the Salt Lake Valley for several years, then moved south to the village of Parowan. On September 11, 1857, he helped lead a party of some fifty fellow Mormons on an attack of a non-Mormon wagon train, the Fancher party, at Mountain Meadows; 141 men, women, and children were killed. Sir Arthur Conan Doyle used the event as background for his Sherlock Holmes novel, *The Sign of Four*. It is also commemorated in an anti-Mormon song of the time, "The Mormon Bishop's Lament":

> *We marched to Mountain Meadows and on that*
> *   glorious field*
> *With rifle and with hatchet we made man and*
> *   woman yield.*
> *'Twas there we were victorious with our legions*
> *   fierce and brave.*
> *We left the slaughtered victims on the ground*
> *   without a grave.*
> *We slew the load of emigrants on Sublet's lonely*
> *   road,*
> *And plundered many a trader of his then most*
> *   precious load.*

After a brief period in hiding, Lee returned to Parowan and lived there until 1870, when Young warned him that the federal government was at last taking action against those who had participated in the slaughter. Young ordered Lee to move to Kanab, fifty miles from the North Rim of the Grand Canyon, and the next year dispatched Lee to the Colorado River crossing at Lonely Dell, which soon became known as Lees Ferry. There Lee, using a wooden boat that John Wesley Powell left with him, took passengers and freight from shore to shore, confident that the remote location would keep him and his wives well away from the national government. Remote it was, too; when Arizona's first governor, George Hunt, visited Lees Ferry, he is said to have remarked, "Hell, if I had to live in this place, I'd want more than one wife myself!"

On November 7, 1874, Lee was arrested in Panguitch, Utah, where one of his wives lived. Young had excommunicated Lee, making it easier for the all-Mormon jury to find him guilty of murder. As he had for years, Lee protested his innocence—

according to explorer Frederick Dellenbaugh, those protestations had earned him the nickname Naguts, "crybaby," among local Paiutes—but to no avail. On March 9, 1877, Lee was executed by firing squad at the site of the Mountain Meadows Massacre, the only participant in the crime to be so punished.

Lees Ferry, standing at the confluence of the Paria and Colorado Rivers, marks Mile 0 (see 140 Mile Canyon) on maps of the Colorado River through the Grand Canyon. (Before the completion of Boulder Dam, now called Hoover Dam, those river miles numbered 277; with the formation of Lake Mead, forty miles were lost.) Fray Vélez de Escalante described the area in his 1776 report, saying of the Echo Cliffs Monocline below which the ferry lies that "it has a pleasantly confused appearance," and noting of the area,

> . . . the descent to the river is very long, steep, rugged, and precipitous, consisting of such terrible rock embankments that two pack animals which descended the first one could not make it back, even without the equipment. . . . The river was very deep, although not as much as at Salsipuedes, but the horse herds had to swim for a long distance. The good thing about it is that it was not quicksand, either going in or getting out. The companions kept insisting that we should descend to the river, since there was no way on the other side to go ahead after one crossed the river, except a deep and narrow canyon of another small one which joins it here—and since we had not learned if this one could be negotiated or not—we feared finding ourselves obliged (if we went down and crossed the river) to do the necessary back tracking which on the precipice would be extremely difficult.

Lee Canyon downriver, below Supai, also bears Lee's name.

LINDBERGH HILL

This small North Rim rise bears the name of Charles A. Lindbergh (1902–1974), the famed American aviator whose solo transatlantic flight in 1927 excited international attention.

LIPAN POINT

The Lipan Apaches are a Texas tribe whose territory lies far from the Grand Canyon. This point was until 1902 named Lincoln Point after the American president; the cartographer François Matthes requested the change for unknown reasons.

LITTLE COLORADO RIVER

Also called the Colorado Chiquito and Río de Lino (River of Flax), this small river carries what in toponymastics is called a "tributary diminutive." The Little Colorado rises in the White Mountains of Arizona above the hamlet of Greer and flows into the Colorado.

On August 10, 1869, John Wesley Powell stopped at the mouth of the Little Colorado below Marble Canyon and considered what his impending trip into the Inner Gorge might bring:

> We are three-quarters of a mile in the depths of the earth, and the great river shrinks into insignificance, as it dashes its angry waves against the walls and cliffs, that rise to the world above; they are but puny ripples, and we but pigmies, running up and down the sands, or lost among the boulders. We have an unknown distance yet to run; an unknown river yet to explore. What falls there are, we know not; what rocks beset the channel, we know not; what walls rise over the river, we know not.

LOOKOUT POINT

This designation, for a point off the Hermit Trail between Santa Maria Springs (q.v.) and Breezy Point (q.v.), given by the United States Geographical Survey in 1906, is perhaps the least inventive descriptor in the Canyon's roster of place names.

LYELL BUTTE

Sir Charles Lyell (1797–1875) was an English geologist who may be ranked among the most influential scientists in history. A champion of the theory of uniformitarianism, which holds that all geological phenomena are the result of regular and predictable processes of erosion, decay, deposition, and stratification, he also gave early and important support to Charles Darwin's theories of evolution (*see* Darwin Plateau). Lyell's *Principles of Geology* (1830–33) went into twelve editions in his lifetime. In it, Lyell proposed a geological timetable that includes the designations Eocene, Miocene, and Pliocene epochs, which remain standard today. It is entirely appropriate that this geological wonderland should harbor a feature honoring Lyell, for every early geologist who explored the Canyon region was steeped in his work.

MAIDEN'S BREAST

George Wharton James named this rock formation at Maricopa Point (*q.v.*), writing that the Havasupai Indians had suggested it for "a small nipple in the sandstone." George Stewart, author of *American Place-Names*, has noted that the human breast has given many landscape features across the world their names, including, famously, that of the Grand Teton Mountains. In the Southwest, one finds the abundant toponym "Molly's Nipple" and several variants; one such Mollies Nipple lies off Whitmore Canyon on the North Rim. (Whoever Molly was, she evidently got around.) In the nineteenth century the name "maiden" was also attached, with ironic intent, to zones of prostitution, such as San Francisco's notorious Maiden Lane.

MALAGOSA CANYON

This narrow canyon in the eastern park bears the name of Pedro de Malgosa (also Melgosa and Maigosa), a sergeant in Cárdenas's detachment (*see* Cárdenas Butte) who managed to descend several hundred feet into the Canyon before being forced to turn back.

MALLERY GROTTO

Also Mallery's Grotto. This cave in the El Tovar Amphitheater was named for Garrick Mallery, a specialist in Native American pictography, who had made studies of the area. The cave contains numerous Havasupai rock paintings.

MANU TEMPLE

The English traveler and writer George Wharton James named this 7,181-foot bluff after Manu, the legendary Hindu lawgiver.

MANZANITA POINT

John White, a resident of the North Rim in the mid-1920s, named this projection for the manzanita (*Arctostaphylos manzanita*) bushes that grow nearby. The name, which in Spanish means "little apple," refers to the shrub's berrylike fruit.

MARBLE CANYON

John Wesley Powell (*see* Powell Plateau) named this canyon on the Colorado River on August 9, 1869, writing, "The walls of the cañon, 2,500 feet high, are of marble, of many beautiful colors, often polished below by the waves. . . . As this great bed forms a distinctive feature of the cañon, we call it Marble Cañon." Also called Marble Gorge, Marble Canyon ends at Mile 61.5, the confluence of the Colorado and Little Colorado Rivers.

MARCOS TERRACE

United States Geological Survey maps show this feature by this name beginning in 1927. The Marcos in question is Fray Marcos de Niza (*see* Coronado Butte). Explorers Monument lies below the southern end of the terrace.

MARICOPA POINT

Named in 1906 by the Board of Geographic Names, Maricopa Point honors the Maricopa Indians of central Arizona, who farmed along the Gila River. The name is thought to be a transposition of the Spanish *mariposa*, butterfly, a reference to the Maricopas' painted faces.

MARION POINT

John H. Marion (1835–1891) was a Prescott publisher who launched Arizona's first English-only campaign in his newspaper, the *Arizona Miner*, in which, John Gregory Bourke (*see* Bourke Point) recalls, "not so much as a Spanish advertisement could be found." The historian Will Croft Barnes bestowed the name of this 5,300-rise above Nankoweap Canyon.

MARSH BUTTE

English-born writer and traveler George Wharton James named this rise after O. Charles Marsh, a Yale professor of paleontology who extensively studied the remains of *Eohippus* and other ancestral horses while serving as director of the vertebrate paleontology section of the United States Geological Survey. Before 1906, it was called Endymion Dome, after the boy of Greek mythology whom Selene, the moon goddess, loved.

MASONIC TEMPLE

George Wharton James is thought to have named this bluff for the Order of Freemasons, an anticlerical organization to which he belonged. However, the Masonic Mine in Mono County, California, was famed throughout the West at the time, and the name may have been given by association.

MATHER POINT

Stephen T. Mather (1867–1930) was the first director of the National Park Service. A wealthy man thanks to shrewd mining investments, he personally paid for several improvements in Grand Canyon National Park. Mather Pass, in Kings Canyon National Park, also bears his name.

Taking in the view from then-unnamed Mather Point, the French general Ferdinand Foch, commander of the Allied forces in World War I, was transfixed by the Canyon's immensity. After gazing silently for long minutes, he turned to his American escort and exclaimed, "What a wonderful place to drop one's mother-in-law!"

MATKATAMIBA CANYON

This extremely narrow redwall canyon, which Colin Fletcher calls "a deep, many-armed monster" above Upset Rapid (q.v.), takes its name from a Havasupai family. Canyon habitués often refer to it by the shortened form Matkat.

In his book *The River That Flows Uphill*, neuroscientist William Calvin remarks,

> *If I ever made a fortune, I'd have a landscape architect copy this magical place, right down to the desert plants that surround it, and have it installed somehow in my back yard. Unfortunately, it would require a crew of gardeners to maintain. But Matkat manages nicely without help, because each of the ingredients has been selected by the environment over the centuries to work together with the others. It is a small ecosystem that cannot readily be transported elsewhere.*

MATTHES POINT

François Emile Matthes (1874–1948), a Flemish immigrant, was appointed in 1902 to make a U.S. government topographic map of the Grand Canyon region. With some assistance from Richard T. Evans, he mapped the Vishnu, Bright Angel, Shinumo, and Supai sectors. While doing so, he assigned many of the place names the Canyon now bears, often using what explorer Frederick Dellenbaugh called "Dutton's heroic nomenclature."

McKEE POINT

The name of this overlook above the Colorado River in the Hualapai Indian Reservation honors Edwin D. McKee, a distinguished student of Grand Canyon geology.

MENCIUS TEMPLE

Mencius is the latinized form of Meng Tse (ca. 372–288 B.C.), who codified the Confucian laws in the *Analects*. Meng Tse was not easily impressed by landscape, remarking of China's most sacred mountain, "Ta'i Shan is the same as small mounds of dirt." The early Canyon surveyor Clarence Dutton is the probable author of the name.

MERLIN ABYSS

Cartographer Richard T. Evans named this canyon after the famous sorcerer of the Arthurian cycle of legends.

MESCALERO POINT

This overlook takes its name from the Mescalero Apache, a tribe living in the mountains of south-central New Mexico. The name comes from *mescal*, a kind of agave that served as a major food source for many desert peoples. Its sap, when fermented, yields a potent alcoholic drink, also called *mescal*.

MILLET POINT

Historian Will Croft Barnes attributes the origin of this name to a commemorative for Frank Millet (b. 1846), a noted landscape artist who died in the sinking of the *S.S. Titanic* in 1912. Why Millet should be so honored is not clear.

MIMBREÑO POINT

This point takes its name from the Mimbres Apache, a tribe that lived along the Mimbres River, a tributary of the Gila, in southern New Mexico.

MODRED ABYSS

The Welsh cartographer Richard T. Evans named this chasm after Modred (also spelled Mordred), who murdered King Arthur.

MOHAVE POINT

The Mojave Indians historically lived along the lower Colorado River in the vicinity of Needles, California, and most now live farther down the river near Parker, Arizona. As a rule, the spelling of the word in place names is Mojave in California and Mohave in Arizona.

MONADNOCK AMPHITHEATER

The United States Geological Survey called this hollow near Emerald Canyon for the technical term for a vestigial hill left after a plateau has been scraped away by erosion.

MONTEZUMA POINT

The name of this point, at the eastern end of Aztec Amphitheater (*q.v.*), honors the last emperor of the Aztecs, whom the Spanish conquistador Hernán Cortez overthrew in 1520.

MONUMENT CREEK

John Wesley Powell named this South Rim stream (*see* The Abyss) in 1883, although exactly what he wished to commemorate is unclear. Some writers believe the name refers to a hundred-foot-tall rock pinnacle in the creekbed. There are dozens of such "monument rocks" on maps of the Colorado Plateau.

MOONEY FALLS

Mooney Falls takes its name from Daniel W. Mooney, a prospector who fell to his death near there in 1880 while trying to descend a cliff face by rope during his search for minerals in lower Havasu Canyon. According to some accounts Mooney's rope was caught on a rock snag, and he dangled for two days before finally plunging 200 feet to his death.

MORAN POINT

Thomas Moran accompanied the Wheeler Survey to Yellowstone as an artist in 1871. He first came to the Grand Canyon in 1873 at the invitation of John Wesley Powell; there he made the "Chasm of the Colorado" and other famous illustrations. He returned in

1880 to illustrate Clarence Dutton's *Tertiary History of the Grand Canyon District*. Influenced by James McNeil Whistler, Moran made paintings that, although certainly beautiful, are not altogether faithful to physical reality; he thought little of rearranging nature to suit his artistic ideas. However, at an exhibit of his paintings in 1917 he said that the Canyon had taught him that "the business of the great painter should be the representation of great scenes in nature." Most of Moran's paintings were made from the vantage point of Powell Plateau (*q.v.*).

Ellsworth Kolb has written, "Thomas Moran's name, more than any other, with the possible exception of Major Powell's, is to be associated with the Grand Canyon." It is fitting that 7,157-foot Moran Point, on the East Rim, should be a favorite of artists and photographers.

MUAV CANYON

Muav is a Paiute word meaning "divide" or "saddle," and this 5,000-foot pass divides the North Rim from Powell Plateau. The 200-foot-thick Muav Limestone deposit throughout the eastern canyon is about 450 million years old; a reddish-stained gray formation, it lies between Bright Angel Shale and Redwall Limestone.

NAJI POINT

Pioneer historian and writer Will Croft Barnes named this point after Naji (also Naiche or Natchi, as nearby Natchi Canyon is named), one of the sons of the Chiricahua Apache leader Cochise (*see* Cochise Butte). Naji is overshadowed in history by the shaman Geronimo; as one elderly Apache remarked to a reporter, "Naiche was not a Medicine Man, so he needed Geronimo as Geronimo needed him." This is commonly referred to as Uncle Jim Point (*q.v.*).

NANKOWEAP CANYON

Ann Haymond Zwinger writes in *Downcanyon* that John Wesley Powell "named Nankoweap using a Paiute name of rather confused etymology, but never mind: it's a euphonious name and a beautiful place." Some writers claim that the word is a Paiute phrase meaning "place where people were killed" in commemoration of a Navajo raid in which several Paiutes died, and such a raid did occur near Nankoweap Canyon. The early canyon explorer Frederick Dellenbaugh traces the word to a phrase, also Paiute, that means something like "place that echoes"; Nankoweap Canyon certainly does that. The element *weap* itself means canyon or wash. Whatever the etymology, the cartographer François Matthes so named Nankoweap Canyon in 1927.

NAVAJO POINT
Named after the nearby Indian nation, 7,461-foot Navajo Point, on the East Rim Drive, is the highest elevation on the South Rim.

NAUTILOID CANYON
This small canyon at Mile 34.8 contains the fossil remnants of several types of nautiloids, sea creatures related to squids and octopuses.

NEAL SPRING
This water source at the head of Bright Angel Canyon takes its name from William Neal (1849–1936), an Arizona cattleman and mine operator.

NEWBERRY BUTTE
This 5,104-foot butte is named for John S. Newberry (1822–1892), chief medical officer for the Ives expedition of 1858–59 (*see* Ives Point).

NEWTON BUTTE
This 5,100-foot butte above Boulder Creek is named in honor of the English physicist Isaac Newton (1642–1727), who made several important contributions to early modern science. Reflecting on those contributions, Newton describes himself in terms that visitors feeling insignificant in the face of Grand Canyon's vastness can appreciate:

*I do not know what I may appear to the world; but to myself I
seem to have been only like a boy playing on the seashore, and
diverting myself now and then finding a smoother pebble or a
prettier shell than ordinary, while the great ocean of truth lay
undiscovered before me.*

NOVINGER BUTTE

Frank Bond (*see* Alsap Butte) named this butte after Simon
Novinger (1832–1904), an early settler in the Salt River Valley
who spent much of his later life searching for the legendary Lost
Dutchman Mine in the Superstition Mountains east of Phoenix.
On that matter, the noted Southwestern writer Mary Austin observes, "the palpable sense of mystery in the desert air breeds
fables, chiefly of lost treasure. . . . Old miners drifting about the
desert's edge, weathered into the semblance of tawny hills, will
tell you tales like these convincingly. After a little sojourn in that
land you will believe them on their own account. It is a question
whether it is not better to be bitten by a little horned snake of
the desert that goes sideways and strikes without coiling than by
the tradition of a lost mine."

OBI POINT

Crossword puzzle fans know that an *obi* is the sash for a kimono,
but the origin of this North Rim point's name is in the Paiute
word for a local pinyon pine, *Pinus edulis.*

OCHOA POINT

Estevan Ochoa (1831–1888) was an immigrant from Chihuahua
who operated several businesses in and served as mayor of Tucson. Frank Bond (*see* Alsap Butte) named this overlook in his
honor.

OLO CANYON

Olo is believed to be a shortened
form of the Havasupai *woólo,*
"horse," from the Spanish *caballo.*
Evidently the Havasupai grazed

their horses in this sometimes grassy canyon, which lies at Mile 145 between Kanab Creek and Matkatamiba Canyon.

140 MILE CANYON
Claude Birdseye, who explored the Canyon in 1923, established the convention of naming creeks and canyons off the Colorado River for their distance in river miles from Mile 0, Lees Ferry (*q.v.*). He did not follow it consistently, however, for Birdseye also called this Neighing Horse Canyon, a clearly commemorative name.

O'NEILL BUTTE
This 6,071-foot butte is named for William "Buckey" O'Neill (1860–1898), the Yavapai County sheriff who was killed at the Battle of San Juan Hill, the engagement that made Theodore Roosevelt (*see* Roosevelt Point) internationally famous. Arizona historian Will Croft Barnes called O'Neill "brilliant, scholarly, but very eccentric."

OSIRIS TEMPLE
Clarence Dutton (*see* Dutton Point) named this 6,637-foot bluff after Osiris, in Egyptian mythology the god of the underworld. Osiris was murdered by his evil brother Set (*see* Tower of Set); his death was avenged by his son Horus.

The pinnacle atop Osiris Temple is composed of the last remnants of an eroded Coconino Sandstone cap. Nearby Isis Temple wears that cap more or less intact.

OTTOMAN AMPHITHEATER
Surveyor Clarence Dutton named this after the Ottoman Empire of Turkey, whose military campaigns in the Balkans were much in the news in the 1880s, and not for this depression's resemblance to a footstool.

OZA BUTTE

In Paiute, *oza* is a kind of narrow-necked basket; this narrow butte resembles one.

PAGUEKWASH POINT

Named after the Paiute word for fishtail, this point has a view of a bifurcated mesa off Fishtail Canyon.

PALISADES OF THE DESERT

This range of 5,000-foot cliffs, running from Cape Solitude (*q.v.*) to Comanche Point (*q.v.*), separates the Painted Desert from the eastern Grand Canyon. The descriptive name first appears on United States Geological Survey maps in 1886.

PAMAMETA TERRACE

This terrace above Matkatamiba Canyon and below Mount Akaba takes its name from that of a Havasupai family.

PANYA POINT

This point below Supai takes its name from that of a Havasupai family.

PAPAGO POINT

Frank Bond (*see* Alsap Butte) named this South Rim projection for the Papago Indians, as they were then called, of southern Arizona and northern Sonora. *Papawi* or *babawi*, in the language of the Opata Indians of Mexico, means "bean eaters," and refers to the widespread indigenous use of mesquite pods and tepary beans. The Papago call themselves *Tohono O'odham*, "people of the stony ground," which perfectly describes their Sonoran Desert homeland.

Papago Point also bears the name Hollenbeck Point, after two sisters who visited John Hance (*see* Hance Creek) a century ago. The Board of Geographic Names evidently now favors Hollenbeck Point, to judge by recently issued maps, although Papago Point—or better, Tohono O'odham Point—is to be preferred.

PARASHONT CANYON

Also Parashunt and Parashant. Two ety-
mologies from the Paiute have been proposed for the origin of this rugged canyon's
name, the one meaning "much water," the
other meaning "elk hide." Given the abundance of both water and elk in the canyon,
either one makes sense.

PARISSAWAMPITTS POINT

Clarence Dutton, the famed Canyon surveyor, named this point
above Tapeats Creek on the North Rim, mistranscribing a Paiute
phrase meaning "place where the water bubbles." A spring of
the same name is the source of water.

PATTIE BUTTE

In the early fall of 1824 a party of American trappers followed
the Santa Fe Trail from Council Bluffs, Iowa, to its terminus in
New Mexico. They were the first Anglos to have approached the
capital in eighteen years; Lieutenant Zebulon Pike, surveying the
new lands of the Louisiana Purchase, had been jailed there in
1806 on the charge of espionage. (The mayor released him with
the proviso that Pike get out of Spanish territory at once. Pike
did.) On arriving in Santa Fe the Americans met with the Mexican governor, who granted them a license to trap beaver along
the Gila River. The drainage was still largely unknown, and the
governor reasoned that he might be able to attain a more or less
accurate geographical survey of the region at the cost of a few pelts
to the Mexican treasury.

Among the party's number was young James Ohio Pattie,
the son of its leader, Sylvester Pattie. James Ohio Pattie had a
keen eye for the details of the landscape if an overly heightened
sense of exaggeration, and his *Personal Narrative*, ghostwritten
by newspaper editor Timothy Flint of Cincinnati and first published in 1831, remains an interesting but wholly untrustworthy
source of information. The following passage may describe the
Colorado, or "Red," River. If it does—and scholars have debated

the location for years—it means that Pattie was the first citizen of
the United States to see the Grand Canyon.

*On the 25th we reached a small stream, emptying into Red river
through the east bank, up which we detached three men, each
carrying a trap, to discover if beavers abounded in that stream.
They were to return the next day, while we were engaged in shoe-
ing our horses. The next day elapsed, but none returned. We
became anxious about their fate; and on the 27th, started to see
what had become of them. At mid-day we found their bodies cut
in pieces, and spitted before a great fire, after the same fashion
which is used in roasting beaver. The Indians who had murdered
them, saw us as we came on, and fled to the mountains, so that
we had no chance of avenging the death of our unfortunate companions. We gathered the fragments of their bodies together and
buried them. With sadness in our hearts, and dejection on our
countenances, we returned to our camp, struck our tents, and
marched on. The temperature in this region is rather severe, and
we were wretchedly clad to encounter the cold.*

*On the 28th, we reached a point of the river where the
mountains shut in so close upon its shores, that we were com-
pelled to climb a mountain, and travel along the acclivity, the
river still in sight, and at an immense depth beneath us.—
Through this whole distance, which we judged to be, as the river
meanders, 100 leagues, we had snow from a foot to eighteen
inches deep. . . . April 10th, we arrived where the river emerges
from these horrid mountains, which so cage it up, as to deprive
all human beings of the ability to descend to its banks, and make
use of its waters.*

James Ohio Pattie later joined another trapping party organized
by the Robidoux brothers of St. Louis. He never found his fortune, and he eventually returned to his native Kentucky, where
he died in the great cholera epidemic of 1833 at the age of twenty-
nine. The name of this 4,200-foot rise below Newton Butte (*q.v.*)
honors his memory.

PAYA POINT

This point takes its name from that of a Havasupai family. Lemuel Paya was a tribal spokesman during negotiations over the boundaries of the Havasupai Reservation.

PESHLAKAI POINT

The name of this point, which juts out from the Palisades of the Desert (*q.v.*), honors an important modern Navajo silversmith.

PHANTOM RANCH

Mary Elizabeth Jane Colter, an architect who worked for the Fred Harvey Company, named this locale after nearby Phantom Creek, itself apparently named for the romantic associations the word "phantom" evokes. (*See also* Haunted Canyon.) Founded in 1903 as a camp for hunting parties, the ranch stood near David Rust's aerial tramway over the Colorado and near the junction of several inner-canyon trails. It was later named Roosevelt's Camp after Theodore Roosevelt visited the spot to dedicate a suspension bridge over the Colorado River in 1913, a visit Marguerite Henry commemorates in her children's novel *Brighty of the Grand Canyon*. The Fred Harvey Company built the present "ranch" as a tourist resort in 1922, and the appellation Phantom has endured.

PIMA POINT

Also called Hermit Point (*see* Boucher Creek), this West Rim point honors the Pima Indians of southern Arizona. In the language of the Akimel O'odham, or "watercourse people," their proper name, *pim'ach*, means "I don't understand you." This was very likely the response received by the first Spanish conquistador to ask "*¿Quién es usted?*"—"Who are you?"

PINAL POINT

The Pinal (Spanish for "pine-clad mountain") Apaches lived in the mountains of south-central Arizona until their removal to the San Carlos Apache Reservation. No longer a distinct ethnic group, they are remembered in the name of this South Rim overlook and by the name of a county and mountain range in southern Arizona.

PIPE CREEK

Ralph Cameron, for whom the town of Cameron, Arizona, is named, found a meerschaum pipe near this old mining trail in 1894 and, as a hoax, carved a date on it placing it in the early 1800s. He put it along the trail for other members of his party to find. Cameron's trick fooled his friends, including Peter Berry (see Grandview Point), until he owned up to it, and it yielded the incident name Pipe Creek. The stream follows Pipe Creek Fault, a part of the Bright Angel Fault system.

PIUTE POINT

This point honors the indigenous people of the North Rim, properly spelled Paiute, which means "water people."

POINT CENTEOTL

The derivation of this Aztec term and its authorship as a place name for a point off Aztec Amphitheater are both uncertain. Some writers hazard the guess that it is a misrendering of the Nahuatl *coyotl*, "coyote." It would be a happier accident if the term were taken from that language's *centlani*, "in the abyss."

POINT HUITZIL

The Huitzil, more commonly known as the Huichol, are an Indian tribe of west-central Mexico. As with Point Centeotl above, the authorship of this place name is not known.

POINT IMPERIAL

At 8,803 feet, this point is the highest on either rim of the Grand Canyon, yielding its regal name. The Colorado River is exactly 6,600 feet below Point Imperial.

POINT QUETZAL

The *quetzal* is a Central American bird whose plumage was much valued as a trade item among the native peoples of the Colorado Plateau.

POINT RETREAT

Robert Stanton named this 3,000-foot rise in Marble Canyon after using the point opposite as an escape route following the 1889 drownings of Frank M. Brown, Peter Hansbrough, and Henry Richards. Vascys Paradise (*q.v.*) lies immediately below.

POINT SUBLIME

Sublime is a word that often appears in the Canyon writings of Clarence Dutton, who named this, one of his favorite spots in the Grand Canyon, in 1880. Calling it "one of the most sublime of earthly spectacles," he used this overlook as a touchstone for his famed descriptions of the Canyon. "The scenery of the amphitheatre," he elaborates,

> *far surpasses in grandeur anything else of the kind in any other region. . . . The supreme views are to be obtained at the extremities of the long promontories which jut out between these recesses far into the gulf. Towards such a point we now direct our steps. The one we have chosen is on the whole the most commanding in the Kaibab front, though there are several others which might be regarded as very nearly equal to it, or as even more imposing in some respects. We named it Point Sublime.*

POLLUX TEMPLE

See Castor Temple.

POSTON BUTTE

Charles Debrille Poston (1825–1902) is known as the "father of Arizona," although others are more worthy of the title. Poston came to Arizona in 1854, when he and Hermann Ehrenberg (*see* Ehrenberg Point) founded Colorado City, which later became

Yuma. Poston moved to Tucson in 1856 and operated several mining ventures with mixed success. Having conceived political ambitions, he served as superintendent of Indian affairs for Arizona Territory during the Civil War, and then held various posts abroad. He died in extreme poverty in Phoenix in 1902 and is buried in a pyramid tomb on a small butte just west of Florence, Arizona.

POWELL PLATEAU

The famed explorer and ethnologist John Wesley Powell (1834–1902) is responsible for the names of dozens of points in the Grand Canyon region, and hundreds across the West. Yet, modestly, he gave none of them his own name. It was up to later admirers to name this island plateau after him, as well as the huge lake that formed behind Glen Canyon Dam after its completion in 1963 and a few other spots on the map of the Colorado Plateau. Powell Mountain, in Kings Canyon National Park, California, also bears his name.

The northern point of Powell Plateau is at this writing unnamed. Stephen J. Pyne, a longtime student of Canyon history, has proposed calling it Gilbert Point, after G. K. Gilbert, a geologist on the Powell and Wheeler surveys. With Powell, Gilbert convened a meeting of the International Congress of Geologists at the Canyon in 1891, the first large-scale scientific convention ever held here.

PRESIDENT HARDING RAPID

Claude Birdseye named this rapid on his river expedition of 1923, the first to benefit from radio contact. Lewis Freeman recalls, in his memoir of the expedition, that the party heard of President Warren G. Harding's death of pneumonia while resting for the evening:

> *Radio had come in as strongly as ever at Badger Creek, but it remained for the thousand-feet-deep section at Soap Creek to furnish a conclusive proof of the utter fallacy of the theory that so profound a natural depression cannot receive from a distance by*

air. Station KHJ had warned us the previous night that it was planning to broadcast us a special lot of messages the evening of August 2nd. That was the night of our arrival at Soap Creek. In preparation for the gala occasion the aerial was carefully set up with one end high on the side of a cliff and orientated on Los Angeles. KHJ came in clearly promptly at 9 o'clock, Mountain Time, with little interference either from static or the crashing roar of the imminent rapid. The lightning of distant thunderstorms was jazzing up the purple wedge of sky between the up-river cliffs but, strangely enough, with scarcely any reaction on the instrument. Baseball scores had come in and the daily grist of news was half way through, when there was a sudden break, followed by a brief space of charged silence. When the announcer resumed, it was to state in a voice of very evident emotion that news had just been received of the death of President Harding in San Francisco. This word was winged a dozen times or more during the next hour, once directly addressed to "the engineers braving the rapids of the Colorado." We had received our special message, though not the one expected.

The first news of the President's death was received about 8:15, Pacific Time—perhaps forty-five minutes after the event. Not one in ten thousand of the city dwellers of the country could have had the news at so early a moment. Col. Birdseye announced at once that a day of rest would be taken by the expedition out of respect to the memory of the President.

PUTESOI CANYON

Also Putesoy. This canyon takes its name from that of a Havasupai family.

RED BUTTE

This 7,600-foot rise on the South Rim bears a purely descriptive name. George Wharton James writes that the Havasupai called it "Hue-ga-da-wi-za, or 'the mountain of the clenched fist.'" (See also Cedar Mountain.)

REDWALL CAVERN

John Wesley Powell (*see* Powell Plateau) named this limestone cavern at Mile 33 descriptively, calling it "a vast half-circular chamber" and saying that it could hold fifty thousand people comfortably. The cavern is far less spacious than Powell suggests.

RIBBON FALLS

This feature, which lies about a third of the way up the Kaibab Trail to the North Rim, was named descriptively: François Matthes (*see* Matthes Point) thought the water flaring in the sunlight resembled ribbons blowing in the breeze. In *Brighty of the Grand Canyon*, Marguerite Henry elaborates, describing the falls as "a white jet of water that shot gaily out of the rocks above, washed down the face of a jutting ledge, and then joined forces with the creek."

ROARING SPRINGS

This North Rim waterfall cascades down a cliff face with such force that the sound can be heard on the rim 3,000 feet above, a happy instance in which a commemorative name actually lives up to fact.

ROOSEVELT POINT

Grand Canyon National Park owes its origins to the efforts of Theodore Roosevelt, a great conservationist under whose presidency it was first protected. For nearly a century, Roosevelt's contributions were not honored with a place name, an astonishing oversight. Thanks to longtime canyon habitué

Jim Babbitt, who took the matter up with the United States Board of Geographic Names, this was remedied in July 1996, when this spit of land off Cape Royal was formally designated Roosevelt Point. As of this writing, it is the newest addition to the national park's map.

ROWES WELL

Sanford Rowe (ca. 1848–1929) was a pioneer stockman on the South Rim who located an underground spring at this point. This also appears on maps as Rowe Well and Rowe's Well.

SADDLE MOUNTAIN

In local parlance, a saddle is a pass be-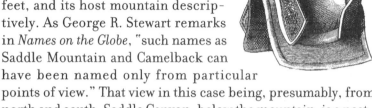
tween two ridges. The explorer Claude
Birdseye named this pass, at 8,425
feet, and its host mountain descriptively. As George R. Stewart remarks
in *Names on the Globe*, "such names as
Saddle Mountain and Camelback can
have been named only from particular
points of view." That view in this case being, presumably, from north and south. Saddle Canyon, below the mountain, is a nesting area of the willow flycatcher *(Empidonax traillii)*, an endangered or threatened species throughout most of its range.

SANTA MARIA SPRINGS

Mary Elizabeth Jane Colter, who named Phantom Ranch (*q.v.*), named this seep to honor the Virgin Mary.

SAPPHIRE CANYON

Sapphire, a semiprecious stone, is found in this western canyon (*see* Agate Canyon).

SCHELLBACH BUTTE

This 6,034-foot mesa is named after Louis Schellbach, chief naturalist at Grand Canyon National Park from 1941 to 1957.

SCYLLA BUTTE

This 4,750-foot butte is named after the sea monster of the Straits of Messina, whom Herakles slew in classical legend. With its partner Charybdis, a rise opposite in Grand Canyon, Scylla also figures as a clanging rock that brought sailors in those straits to a watery grave. Even as a geological feature, why Scylla should rate a place name in the Grand Canyon while Herakles should not is a matter to take up with the proper authorities.

The writer George Wharton James had earlier named this rise Yucatan Peninsula, after the Maya ruins in that Mexican region that were much in the news in the early 1900s, when the Yucatán was also a site of political turmoil. At one point, the Yucatecan government even applied for admission to the United States.

SEPARATION RAPID

Silted in by the formation of Lake Mead, this site is marked by a plaque in the canyon above that reads, "Here on August 28, 1869, Seneca Howland, O. G. Howland, and William H. Dunn separated from the original Powell party, climbed to the North Rim, and were killed by the Indians."

Tensions had been building throughout the 1869 exploration of the Grand Canyon, and they came to a head toward the end of the passage. Jack Sumner, one of the party, told Stanton,

After having had a spat with Howland in the forenoon, Major Powell at the noonday camp informed Dunn that he could leave the camp immediately or pay him fifty dollars a month for rations. . . . As that little statement raised me to a white heat, I interposed and said that if any one voluntarily wished to leave, he could do so, but that no one could be driven from the outfit. Major Powell informed me that he was talking then, and commanding the expedition. I told him that he could talk; all he pleased, but that he must cease then and there, his abuse of Howland and Dunn. Walter Powell tried a bluff and was immediately called to settle, as there was a pretty little sand bar just about long enough for Colt's forty-fours. He replied that he had no arms, and I told him to take his choice of my pistols and choose his distance. He did not accept the proposition. After that little episode, everything went as smooth as with two lovers after

their first quarrel and make-up. Major Powell did not run the
outfit in the same overbearing manner after that. At a portage
or bad let-down he took his geological hammer and kept out of
the way.

The Howland brothers and Dunn did, however, leave the party.
When the Powell party reached a Shivwits Indian camp several
days later they were told, in Mormon scout Jacob Hamblin's
words, that "a number of miners having killed a squaw in a
drunken brawl," the Howlands and Dunn had been ambushed
and killed. Some modern historians believe that Mormons re-
siding in Tocquerville committed the murders because they
feared that the three men were federal agents investigating the
Mountain Meadows Massacre (*see* Lees Ferry), in which those
Mormons had taken part.

Powell himself did not comment on the episode except to
note laconically in his journal, "Boys left us. Ran rapid. Bradley
boat. Made camp on left bank. Camp 44." He later recorded that
the parting was amicable.

SHALER PLATEAU
Nathaniel S. Shaler (1841–1906) taught geology at Harvard Col-
lege for many years while arguing the case for Darwinian evolutionary theory to his colleagues. The Board of Geographic Names
named this 4,200-foot mesa in his honor in 1907.

SHANUB POINT
Shanub is a Paiute word meaning "wild dog." No one is sure why
this point is so named.

SHEBA TEMPLE
This 4,900-foot butte, near Solomon Temple (*q.v.*), is named
after the Biblical land of Sheba, a region of southern Arabia that
embraces modern Yemen, and more particularly its queen. The
Queen of Sheba visited Solomon "to prove him with hard questions" (1 Kings 10), bringing him rare spices, gold, and precious
stones.

SHINUMO ALTAR

Frederick Dellenbaugh, the Canyon explorer, gave this rise, on the east Marble Platform, its descriptive name. He writes that it appeared like "a great altar." He said that a Paiute Indian had told him the cliff-dwelling Anasazi were called, in his language, the Shinumo, although the etymology is uncertain.

In another part of the Canyon, William W. Bass (see Bass Camp) kept an extensive garden along the banks of Shinumo Creek, including fruit trees and grapevines. Robert Stanton (see Stanton Point) planned to build a switching yard there for a railroad that never materialized.

SHIVA TEMPLE

Shiva is the destroyer aspect of the Hindu godhead, for which reason the atomic scientist J. Robert Oppenheimer, on seeing the results of the Trinity nuclear bomb test, recalled the lines from the sacred *Vedas*: "I am Shiva, destroyer of worlds." Clarence Dutton named this jumbled rock complex in 1880, saying, "In such a stupendous scene of wreck it seems as if the fabled 'Destroyer' might find an abode not wholly uncongenial."

The largest of the North Rim buttes, 7,570-foot Shiva Temple rises some 4,000 feet from its base and its top has an area of nearly 300 acres. In 1937, scientists from the American Museum of Natural History scaled it and Wotans Throne (*q.v.*) to study the effects of evolution in isolation. Shiva Temple has been separated from the North Rim mainland for perhaps 100,000 years, and it was thought it would be ecologically analogous to the islandlike *tepuis* of South America. "There is no reason," one expedition member wrote, "why small animals isolated aeons ago should become extinct. . . . If we are able to compare this flora and fauna with that of the Canyon's main rim, we would have a time clock telling us approximately the number of years it has taken to bring back structural change. It will be rolling back the curtain of time to glimpse life as it was in prehistoric days." The island proved little different from the mainland, and the scientists found no evidence of special divergence there. Apart from familiar animals and fossils, however, they did find Anasazi ruins indicating that Shiva Temple had been inhabited by humans for hundreds of years in prehistory. They also found a box of Kodak film, left behind by photographer Emery Kolb on an earlier ascent. Today sport climbers regularly scale Shiva's walls.

SIEBER POINT

Al Sieber (1844–1907) is famous in Arizona history for having served as chief of scouts during the Indian Wars. Born near Heidelberg, Germany, he emigrated to the United States in 1854 and served in the Union army. After the Civil War he went west, working as a packer in the Prescott Valley before returning to military service as a scout in the Apache Wars. Distinguished for heroism under fire—one contemporary remarked, "If ever there was a man who actually did not know physical fear, it was Al Sieber!"—Sieber nonetheless ran afoul of certain officers in the Arizona command and was dismissed in 1890. He died in 1907, crushed by a boulder during the construction of Roosevelt Dam, at which he was a foreman. There is speculation that the boulder was helped along by Apaches working on the dam, but the charge has never been substantiated.

SIEGFRIED PYRE

Siegfried, familiar to devotees of Richard Wagner's Ring cycle of operas, was the mythical prince who stole the treasure of the

Nibelungen. This 7,914-foot mesa lies to the east side of Walhalla Plateau.

SINKING SHIP

R. R. Tillotson, park superintendent in the early 1930s, named this rock formation for its fancied appearance. The earlier name Three Castles is the more suggestive, and in any event the formation is sometimes confused with The Battleship (*q.v.*) on maps.

SINYELLA, MOUNT

Charles Sheldon, a pioneer naturalist in the Southwest, suggested that this mountain and a nearby canyon be named for Sinyella (1853–1923), a prominent Havasupai leader who served as his guide in the fall of 1912. *Sinyella* is the preferred spelling, although *Sinyala* is still found on many maps, as is the name Sinyella Butte.

Writes Sheldon of the mountain, "Tonight the wind is howling and blowing the sand in clouds over us. We have no frying pans or plates, and I am living like an Indian. The Indians call this lone mountain 'Week-eel-eela,' which they say means 'stick sitting up,' a general term for butte."

SOAP CREEK

See Badger Creek.

SOCKDOLAGER RAPID

This rapid, at Mile 79, was named by the explorer John Wesley Powell after the nineteenth-century term for a boxer's knockout punch; he described it as a place "where the rushing waters break into great waves on the rocks, and lash themselves into a mad, white foam." George Flavell, who ran it several years after Powell, wrote, "This [rapid] was very long, some five or six hundred yards, and with a fall of at least 25 feet. . . . At the head of the rapid we ran over a sunken boulder, and as her bow went down between the next wave, some suction seemed to hold it down, some undercurrent, and the wave broke clear over. I never saw the like before."

SOLOMON TEMPLE

Lying near Sheba Temple (*q.v.*), this 5,070-foot butte honors the legendary tenth-century B.C. king of Israel, builder of the great temple at Jerusalem. Solomon was noted throughout the ancient Near East for his wisdom and generosity.

SPECTER TERRACE

The name of this terrace below Powell Plateau was proposed to the United States Geological Survey in the early 1900s, although by whom it is not certain. It may have been formed by analogy with Phantom Creek and Haunted Canyon; some writers suggest that the dark schist that lines Specter Canyon hinted at the supernatural, although this seems a bit of a stretch.

SPENCER TERRACE

Herbert Spencer (1820–1903) was a leading proponent of what has come to be called Social Darwinism, a belief in the endless progress and perfectibility of species, not least of them human beings. Spencer coined the phrase "survival of the fittest" as shorthand for Charles Darwin's ideas of natural selection.

Spencer Terrace is believed to mark the northern range of the cactus wren *(Campylorhynchus brunneicapillus)*, Arizona's state bird.

SPOONHEAD, MOUNT

This western peak, 5,775 feet high, was named after a Havasupai unceremoniously called Spoonhead by an Indian agent who employed him.

STANTON POINT

Robert Brewster Stanton surveyed the Grand Canyon in 1889 and 1890 for the Denver, Colorado Canyon, and Pacific Railroad, planning a railroad that was never built. His river survey was disastrous—several of his companions drowned, and he himself could not swim—but he nonetheless completed the survey, exposing more than 2,200 film negatives of sites along the whole Canyon. Those photographs are still used as a baseline for rephotographic surveys, which compare features of the landscape against photographs of those features from earlier years.

Stanton's Cave, at Mile 31.8, offers the earliest evidence of human habitation in the Canyon in the form of split-twig figurines of deer and bighorn sheep. These figurines, artifacts of what the mythographer Sir James Frazer called "sympathetic magic," were made of single willow twigs, bent to form representations of the ancient hunters' prey; sometimes another twig pierced them, as if to represent a spear that had found its mark. No other evidence of occupation appears in the cave, suggesting that it was used only for religious purposes. The cave, 200 feet deep and as high as 50 feet in places, also contains the bones of long-extinct birds and a species of camel. One of those bird species, *Teratornis merriami*, is the gigantic ancestor of the California condor. Another condor, *Gymnogyps amplus*, survived in the Canyon until 1881, when prospectors killed the last member of the species.

Giant birds may soon wing their way over the Canyon again. In the winter of 1996 scientists from the Peregrine Fund released six California condors at the Vermilion Cliffs, not far from the national park's northeastern entrance. One died, but the other five appear to be adapting well to their species' former habitat.

STEPHEN AISLE

The section of the Colorado River between Miles 117 and 119, visible from Marcos Terrace (*q.v.*) is named Stephen Aisle in commemoration of Estévanico, the Moorish traveler (*see* Coronado Butte, De Vaca Terrace). It would be better named Estévanico Aisle, but its unknown namer chose the anglicized form for reasons unknown.

STONE CREEK
Entering the Colorado at Mile 132, this creek was named for Julius Stone, a manufacturer of firefighting equipment who lived in Columbus, Ohio. In 1909, Stone set out to follow John Wesley Powell's passage through Grand Canyon. He put in at Green River, Wyoming, on September 12, and left the river at Needles, California, on November 19, a journey he recounts in his entertaining book *Canyon Country*.

STURDEVANT POINT
Glen E. Sturdevant, the first officially appointed naturalist of Grand Canyon National Park, drowned in 1929 near Horn Creek (*see also* Johnson Point). Edwin D. McKee, his successor, suggested this name in Sturdevant's memory.

SULLIVAN POINT
Will Croft Barnes, the Arizona writer and historian, named this rise near Point Imperial after J. W. Sullivan (1844–1923), a prominent Prescott Valley rancher.

SUMNER BUTTE
Frank Bond (*see* Alsap Butte) named this butte after John C. Sumner, a hunter and trapper with John Wesley Powell's first Canyon expedition.

SURPRISE VALLEY
A classic incident name. While strolling near their riverside campsite, E. O. Beaman, the photographer on Powell's second Canyon expedition, found this hanging valley between Deer Creek and Thunder River. It cannot be seen from the Colorado River, hence Beaman's choice of name.

SWILLING BUTTE
John Swilling has been called "the father of Phoenix." A born adventurer, he had drifted eastward from Gila City in 1858, spied for the Confederacy, and organized the so-called Gila Rangers in 1864 to fight the Yavapai Apaches. Swilling recognized that

the ancient ditches in the Phoenix area were irrigation canals built by the prehistoric Hohokam people, and he restored several miles' worth to sell to newcomer farmers. The original townsite he founded, not far from where Sky Harbor International Airport now stands, was first given the moniker Swillings Mill. Swilling later suggested that the growing town be called Stonewall, after the nickname for Confederate general Thomas Jonathan Jackson. His fellow citizens, however, mindful of the depredations Tucson suffered for having sided with the Southern cause, tabled Swilling's motion. He made a good sum of money selling lots in what would become Phoenix (*see* Duppa Point), but addictions to laudanum and alcohol depleted his purse, and in 1878 he unsuccessfully tried to rob a Butterfield stagecoach. Locked up in the Yuma Territorial Prison, Swilling died of typhus at the age of forty-seven, still nursing dreams of creating a canal city to rival Venice. Frank Bond (*see* Alsap Butte) named this point after the star-crossed pioneer.

THE TABERNACLE
In classical usage, a tabernacle is a portable altar such as the one that Moses and his people carried into the wilderness. That naming conforms nicely to this 4,830-foot rise's location just above Solomon Temple.

TAHUTA POINT
The Board of Geographical Names awarded this name in 1925 to honor Eunice Tahuta Jones (1876–1964), a Havasupai leader. The concession was unusual, given that the board does not like to assign names in honor of living persons.

TANNER CANYON
Seth B. Tanner was a Mormon pioneer who ran a trading post at Moenkopi, on the Hopi Reservation. In 1880 he staked claims to several mines along the Colorado River and built a system of trails to reach them. That system was also called the Horsethief Trail; it was used by a gang of rustlers who operated between southern Arizona and southern Utah, crossing the Colorado at this point

below the East Rim. At this writing, the Park Service plans to maintain the Tanner Trail, which it had not done before.

TAPEATS CREEK

John Wesley Powell named this creek and its associated terrace, amphitheater, and cave for Ta Pits, a Paiute who showed Powell the creek from a point on the North Rim, saying he owned it.

Frederick Dellenbaugh, a member of the second Powell expedition into the Canyon, writes, "A morning [September 6, 1872] was spent at Tapeats Creek for examinations, and we found there some ancient house ruins not far up the side canyon. I discovered a fine large metate or Indian mill, deeply hollowed out, and foolishly attempted to take it to camp. On arriving there it was so heavy I had to drop it and it broke in two, much to the Major's disgust, who told me I ought to have let it alone, a fact which I realized then also."

TEMPLE BUTTE

Given the meaning of the term *temple* in Grand Canyon usage—as a synonym for *butte*—the name of this 5,300-foot mesa in the eastern Canyon is an unfortunate pleonasm whose perpetrator is unknown.

THOMPSON CANYON

This high North Rim canyon takes its name from Charles Thompson, a cattleman who operated V. T. Ranch (*see* De Motte Park).

THOMPSON POINT

This 6,570-foot elevation was named for Dr. Almon Harris Thompson, a geographer with John Wesley Powell's second Canyon expedition who also happened to be Powell's brother-in-law.

THOR TEMPLE

In keeping with the tendency of the time to name Grand Canyon locales after figures of world mythology and literature, the writer

George Wharton James named a rock formation nearby because of its hammerlike appearance—a hammer large enough, he fancied, to have been carried by the Norse war god Thor. The butte above was named by extension.

THUNDER RIVER

Descriptively named, like Roaring Springs (*q.v.*), after the rushing waterfall that lies upstream of the confluence with Tapeats Creek and the Colorado River, the Thunder River is only half a mile long. It is one of the shortest, if not the shortest, named rivers in the world.

TILTED MESA

The cartographer François Matthes suggested the descriptive name for this sloping formation west of Marble Gorge. Earlier writers also referred to it as "the Tilts" and "Tilted Plateau."

TITIHUMJI POINT

This point takes its name from that of a Havasupai family, also rendered as Tithumigi.

TIYO POINT

Tiyo is a hero in Hopi mythology who traversed the Canyon on a cottonwood log, hoping to find out where the river went, with Spider Woman as his guide. His journey took him into the Underworld, where he met Snake Girl, who became his wife and who with him sired the Snake Clan. Tiyo also taught the Hopi people their famous Snake Dance.

Tiyo Point was once called Jupiter Point, representing a successful, and unusual, replacement of an indigenous for a classical place name.

TOLTEC POINT

The Toltec Indians of Mexico, whose empire was conquered by the invading Aztecs from the north, were once erroneously thought to have lived as far north as the Gila River.

TONTO PLATEAU
Until their removal to the San Carlos Reservation in the 1870s, the Tonto Apache lived in north-central Arizona. Their name means "foolish" or "stupid" in Spanish. Some scholars believe that other Apaches gave the group this unhappy name for not resisting the European invaders who came into their territory.

TOPAZ CANYON
The Board of Geographical Names entered this name, probably suggested by cartographer Richard T. Evans, in 1908, commemorating a semiprecious stone found in the area (see Agate Canyon)—but evidently not in this canyon itself.

TOPOCOBA HILLTOP
The name of this rise off Havasu Canyon is somewhat redundant, inasmuch as Topocoba comes from a Havasupai phrase meaning "hilltop water source."

TOROWEAP POINT
Toroweap is a Paiute word meaning "arroyo" or "dry wash." The valley of the same name, leading to this point on the Uinkaret Plateau, is indeed without water for much of the year.

TOVAR TERRACE
On many maps spelled Tobar Terrace. Pedro de Tovar, the scion of a prominent Mexico City family, was a lieutenant on Coronado's expedition of 1540. Hopi Indians told him of the Grand Canyon, but he did not pursue their report, leaving it to Cárdenas to find the Canyon. El Tovar Hotel in Grand Canyon Village, which opened for business in 1905, also bears his name.

TOWAGO POINT
The name of this point over Matkatamiba Canyon is taken from that of a Havasupai family.

TOWER OF BABEL

This name appears in Canyon explorer John Wesley Powell's writings and then all but disappears. It may refer to Vesta Temple, although other writers attach it to other nearby features. It takes its name from the Biblical story (Genesis 11: 1–9) of the Tower of Babel, with which the monolingual citizens of the earth tried to scale the heavens. To punish them for their attempt, God "did confound the language of all the earth," yielding the many tongues that have contributed to the place names of the Grand Canyon.

TOWER OF RA

Thomas Moran, the noted painter, named this 6,076-foot butte in 1879 for Ra, the Egyptian sun god.

TOWER OF SET

Thomas Moran originally named this 6,026-foot butte the Temple of Sett in 1879 because of the niche worn into its wall, which suggested to him temples in the valley of the Nile. Set, so spelled now, was the chief Egyptian god of war and a bitter rival of Osiris (*see* Osiris Temple).

THE TRANSEPT

In classical architecture, the transept is the east-west portion of a cruciform church, crossing its north-south nave. This canyon figuratively crosses Bright Angel Canyon in just such a way. Clarence Dutton named it in 1882, remarking that it was "one of the finest and perhaps most picturesque gorges in the whole Kaibab front."

TRAVERTINE CANYON

Geologist Edwin D. McKee (*see* McKee Point) suggested this descriptive name to commemorate the abundant travertine, a type of limestone, in this area of the western Canyon. Travertine is formed by the deposition of calcium carbonate; many travertine formations in the desert West bear the name "coral," as in Coral Reef, California, near Palm Springs.

In *The Man Who Walked Through Time*, Colin Fletcher writes,

> *I came to Travertine Creek and saw, sure enough, great convoluted slabs of red-brown travertine rock crisscrossing its ravine. The place was dry as a dust bowl; but it was a simple enough matter now for me to picture a blue-green creek tumbling down toward the Inner Gorge, just the way Havasu Creek still tumbled. In its time, this creek too had built convoluted, porcelain-white swimming pools. Then, through some chance flux of geology or climate, the creek had vanished and the white swimming pools had oxidized into bone-dry, red-brown slabs.*

TRINITY CREEK
This small stream at Mile 92 takes its name from the Christian godhead of Father, Son, and Holy Spirit.

TRITLE PEAK
Historian Will Croft Barnes named this rise near Point Imperial for F. A. Tritle, a mining entrepreneur who served as territorial governor of Arizona from 1881 to 1885.

TRUMBULL, MOUNT
Canyon explorer John Wesley Powell named this 8,028-foot peak in the Uinkaret Mountains in honor of the abolitionist Senator Lyman Trumbull (1824–1873). In the summer, Mount Trumbull hosts a large population of western tanagers (*Piranga ludoviciana*), a beautiful songbird.

TUNA CREEK
Tuna refers not to the fish, but is the Spanish name for the fruit of the prickly pear and related plants of the genus *Opuntia*, which grow in abundance here.

TURQUOISE CANYON

Turquoise, a semiprecious stone, is found near but not within this western canyon. The French word means "from Turkey," whence the stone was brought to Europe in the Middle Ages. (*See also* Agate Canyon.)

TUSAYAN RUIN

This Anasazi ruin on the eastern approach to the South Rim dates to about A.D. 1200. It was excavated by Harold S. Gladwin, the noted archaeologist. *Tusayan* is a phonetic rendering of a Hopi phrase meaning "country of isolated buttes," describing the Hopi's aboriginal territory.

TYNDALL DOME

This small rise bears the name of John Tyndall (1820–1893), an English naturalist who helped advance evolutionary theory in his country.

UNCLE JIM POINT

The sources are divided on this name. One school has it that this was named for Uncle Jim Owens (1854?–1936), one of the Canyon's many legendary hermit prospectors. He sometimes worked as a government hunter and is said to have killed more than 1,100 cougars inside the Grand Canyon, thus securing local fame—or infamy, depending on one's point of view. He himself admitted to 533 kills. (Either way, the figures are almost certainly greatly exaggerated.) Uncle Jim also appears as a leading character in Marguerite Henry's novel *Brighty of the Grand Canyon*, where his name is rendered as Owen. In his later years Owens operated a buffalo ranch in House Rock Valley.

Some writers maintain that the point was named for James Pilling, John Wesley Powell's secretary. The first explanation, however, is the likelier. It is also called Naji Point (*q.v.*).

UNKAR CREEK

Unkar comes from the Paiute for "red stone." Anasazi farmers worked the broad delta at the junction of this creek with the

Colorado at Mile 72.5 for several centuries until about A.D. 1150. Ruins dating to that time are found in the immediate vicinity.

UPSET RAPID

On the Geological Survey expedition of 1923, Emery Kolb overturned a boat at this spot eight miles below Kanab Creek, yielding this textbook incident name. Kolb was not injured.

VASEYS PARADISE

Canyon explore Frederick Dellenbaugh writes that John Wesley Powell (*see* Powell Plateau) named this green stretch of shoreline at Mile 32 for "Vasey, the botanist, a friend of his. It was only a lot of ferns, mosses, etc., but it was the first green spot we had seen since leaving the Paria." Powell himself wrote, "The river turns sharply to the east and seems inclosed by a wall set with a million brilliant gems. On coming nearer we find fountains bursting from the rock high overhead, and the spray in the sunshine forms the gems which bedeck the wall. The rocks below the fountain are covered with mosses and ferns and many beautiful flowering plants. We name it Vasey's Paradise, in honor of the botanist who traveled with us last year."

VENUS TEMPLE

Venus, in Roman mythology, was the goddess of love. This 6,257-foot butte lies due east of Cape Final.

VESTA TEMPLE

A member of Clarence Dutton's surveying party, probably Henry Gannett, named this butte after Vesta, the Roman goddess of the hearth.

VIRGIN RIVER

The Virgin River drains much of southwestern Utah and the Arizona Strip, emptying into the Colorado at what is now Lake Mead. Padre Francisco Silvestre Vélez de Escalante, who explored both rims of the Grand Canyon in the fall of 1776, named the river's east fork El Río de Sulfureo for the sulfurous hot springs he found at its headwaters, and so it appears on later Spanish maps of the region. "Here there is a beautiful grove of black poplars, some willow trees, and rambling vines of wild grape," Escalante writes. "Over the space where we backtracked there are ash-strewn areas, veins and other mineral indications, and many rocks smeared with mica." Jedediah Smith, the famed mountain man, surveyed the lower portions of the river in 1827 and named the stream the Adams River in honor of then-president John Adams. Some sources claim, however, that Smith later changed his mind and renamed the river after Thomas Virgen, a member of his party who had been killed not long before in a skirmish with Mojave Indians. The present designation more likely derives from the Virgin Mary, whose name other Spanish explorers often used in assigning names to the places they encountered.

In his *Arizona Place Names*, Will Croft Barnes writes of the small settlement of Bonellis Crossing, at the mouth of the Virgin River: "Bonelli's Ferry consisted of a flat boat which a man pulls across the river with a line. For two persons and a wagon the charge is ten dollars; 50 cents for each additional person. The river can be forded here but is very dangerous."

William R. Palmer, a student of Utah place names, notes that the Paiute word for the Virgin River is *pah-roos*, meaning "'a dirty turbulent stream,' all of which it is. The name is far more fitting than Virgin, which it is not."

VISHNU TEMPLE

Clarence Dutton named this 7,533-foot butte in 1880 after the redeemer aspect of the Hindu godhead. In *Tertiary History of the Grand Canyon District* he writes, "It is a gigantic butte, so admirably designed and so exquisitely decorated . . . and has a surprising resemblance to an Oriental pagoda. We named it Vishnu's Temple." Charles Dudley Warner, a popular writer of the late nineteenth century, elaborates, "The explorers have tried by the use of Oriental nomenclature to bring it within our comprehension, the East being the land of the imagination."

Wallace Stegner, continuing the discussion of exotic place names in the Canyon, remarks in *Beyond the Hundredth Meridian*, "Look at Vishnu's Temple. If you don't call it something like Vishnu's Temple what would you call it? Kwagunt Peak? Ivanpah Butte? . . . Bizarre topography may justify exotic or even eccentric names. . . . In the Grand Canyon, at least, Dutton's names are like his superlatives of description—admissible because they cannot be avoided."

Vishnu Schist, one of the oldest rocks in North America, bears the name of the Temple.

VISTA ENCANTADORA POINT

Grand Canyon National Park supervisor Harold C. Bryant gave this eastern point its name, meaning "enchanting view" in Spanish, in 1941. It is also called Vista Encantada, "enchanted view." In neither case is the name especially inspired.

VULCANS THRONE

Vulcans Throne is the 5,130-foot tall remnant of an ancient volcano at Mile 177. It is not to be confused with Vulcans Anvil, a rock pinnacle a short distance downriver. Vulcan was the Roman god of fire and metallurgy, so the name is unusually appropriate.

WALCOTT BUTTE

The traveler and writer George Wharton James named this feature for Charles D. Walcott, director of the United States Geological Survey and secretary of the Smithsonian Institution from 1907 to 1917. Walcott visited the Canyon in 1882 with John Wesley Powell, his predecessor at the USGS, and helped supervise construction of the Nankoweap Trail.

WALHALLA PLATEAU

Continuing the established pattern of exotic naming, the Flemish cartographer François Matthes dubbed this plateau in 1902 after the legendary mountain fortress of the noble Norse dead. In doing so, he overrode an existing name, Greenland Plateau (*see* Greenland Spring), given to the Plateau by Mormon ranchers. This also appears on early maps as Valhalla Plateau.

WALLACE BUTTE

Alfred Russell Wallace (1823–1913), the English naturalist, arrived independently at ideas of natural selection that supported those of Charles Darwin. Although Darwin's fame eclipsed his own, Wallace is rightly remembered as a founder of evolutionary theory, for which reason this 5,204-foot mesa bears his name.

WALTHENBERG CANYON

John Waltenberg, a colleague of William W. Bass (*see* Bass Camp), helped Levi Noble survey the Shinumo area of the Grand Canyon. Bass once remarked that you could track Waltenberg by the trail of tobacco juice he left behind wherever he went. The misspelling of his name remains by decision of the Board of Geographic Names. It is properly rendered in the place name Waltenberg Rapid, at Mile 112.

WATAHOMIGIE POINT

The name of this overlook near Havasu Canyon is that of a Havasupai family, also spelled Watahomigi and, on some early maps, Warabomigi.

WESCOGAME POINT

The name of this western point is taken from that of a Havasupai family who lived nearby.

WHEELER POINT

Wheeler Point, below Powell Plateau, is named after George Montague Wheeler (1842–1905), an Army officer who surveyed the Grand Canyon region in the 1860s and -70s, It is to him we owe the geographical designation "Colorado Plateau," a term he first used in a report of 1868. His ten-volume *Report upon United States Geographical Surveys West of the One Hundredth Meridian* (1875–1889) remains a standard though criticized source for students of Western exploration. Wheeler abandoned his work after competing surveys led by John Wesley Powell and others received government funding over his own.

WHITES BUTTE

On August 24, 1867, the story has it, prospectors James White, Charles Baker, and Henry Strole attempted a passage of the Colorado River through the Grand Canyon. They were attacked by unidentified Indians (some scholars believe them to have been Utes), and Baker was killed. White and Strole continued, but Strole was washed overboard while negotiating a rapid and drowned. White continued to float downriver for another two weeks until he pulled out at Callville, Utah. Frank Bond (*see* Alsap Butte) named this butte in his honor.

WIDFORSS POINT

Gunnar Mauritz Widforss (1879–1934), a Swedish immigrant, first came to the Canyon in 1921 at the invitation of National Park Service director Stephen T. Mather, who had seen his paintings of Yosemite. Widforss took up residence at the North Rim, and the watercolors he produced, in which the human figure is conspicuously absent, are arguably the best representations of the Grand Canyon in art. At least the director of the National Gallery of Art in Washington thought as much, for which reason many of Widforss's paintings are in its permanent collection. The United States Geographical Board designated this North Rim point in his honor in December 1937.

WODO, MOUNT

According to historian Will Croft Barnes, this elevation bears the name of a Havasupai family who lived on its slopes. The United States Geological Survey proposed the designation in 1925.

WOOLSEY POINT

King S. Woolsey (1832–1879) came to Arizona in 1860 after having spent nearly ten years working as a miner in Calaveras County, California. Woolsey first worked as a teamster in Yuma, saving his money to buy Agua Caliente Ranch in western Maricopa County, on the banks of the Gila River. Although Woolsey, an Alabaman, sympathized with the Confederate cause, he amassed a fortune supplying the Union troops who entered Arizona Territory to secure it for the federal government. Woolsey later established the Agua Fría Ranch near Prescott, where he became famous for organizing attacks on the Yavapai Indians, and especially for an incident in which he poisoned an allotment of pinole with strychnine, killing several innocents. He later turned to ranching and other businesses in the Salt River Valley. Perhaps because of his checkered reputation, Woolsey was defeated in his bid to serve as Arizona's delegate to Congress, but he was nonetheless hailed on his death as a leading citizen of the Territory. For this reason the United States Geographical Board honored him with this place name, along with those of several other locales in Arizona.

WOTANS THRONE

Wotans Throne (also Wotan's Throne) is a 7,633-foot wooded mesa narrowly separated from the North Rim by the forces of erosion. Wotan, or Odin, is the Norse and Germanic god of war. (*See also* Shiva Temple.)

YAKI POINT

Although the circumstances are not entirely clear, the writer George Wharton James seems to have named this 7,260-foot point on the East Rim sometime before 1910 in sympathy for the Yaqui Indians, the objects of a genocidal campaign in their native Mexico throughout the late nineteenth and early twentieth centuries. At the outbreak of the Mexican Revolution of 1910, hundreds of adult Yaqui males were removed to serve as forced labor in the canefields of the Yucatán. Other Yaquis escaped with their families to what was then the Arizona Territory, where they established communities in Tucson and Guadalupe that are extant today. The head of the South Kaibab Trail lies just south of Yaki Point.

YAVAPAI POINT
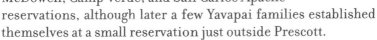
In Paiute, *yavapai* means "sun people," and it designates a group originally distributed widely across central and western Arizona. In the late 1800s, most Yavapai were removed to the Fort McDowell, Camp Verde, and San Carlos Apache reservations, although later a few Yavapai families established themselves at a small reservation just outside Prescott.

YUMA POINT
The United States Geographical Board named this point after the Arizona-California Indian group, whose historical holdings included the site of the present Arizona city (*see* Poston Butte).

YUMTHESKA POINT
According to Arizona writer and historian Will Croft Barnes, this point and its associated mesa were named for a Havasupai family who lived nearby.

YUNOSI POINT
Local legend remembers Yunosi as the wife of the Havasupai chief Hotouta (*see* Hotouta Canyon). After he died, she claimed to receive nightly visits from his ghost, and she would call out to others in her household, "You no see?" This bears all the markings of folk etymology, but the name has stuck.

ZOROASTER TEMPLE

The writer George Wharton James suggested the name of this 7,128-foot butte in 1902 in honor of the Persian religious leader, who lived from

about 660 to 580 B.C. Zoroaster is said to have been born laughing, a sign of divinity. At the age of twenty he left his parents' home to find "the man most in love with righteousness and most disposed to feeding the poor and needy," the best person on Earth. In searching for that man, whom he never found, Zoroaster lived for seven years in a mountain cave alongside the Daiti River of Azerbaijan—territory that, fittingly enough, resembles the Colorado Plateau. There he received visitations from representatives of the god Ahura-Mazda, whose chief holy man he became. Thereafter Zoroaster preached a doctrine of perfection in thought, word, and deed. The sacred text of Zoroastrianism, the *Zend-Avesta*, says that Zoroaster was murdered by an apostate in his seventy-seventh year.

ZUNI POINT

The Zuni people, for whom the United States Geographical Board named this South Rim point, live in western New Mexico. *Zuni* is thought to mean "people of the long fingernails" in the language of Cochiti Pueblo.

BIBLIOGRAPHY

Anderson, Martin J. "Artist in the Wilderness: Frederick Dellenbaugh's Grand Canyon Adventure." *Journal of Arizona History* 28, no. 1 (Spring 1987): 47–68.

Annerino, John. *Hiking the Grand Canyon.* San Francisco: Sierra Club Books, 1986.

Aurousseau, M. *The Rendering of Geographical Names.* London: Hutchinson University Library, 1954.

Austin, Mary. *The Land of Journeys' Ending.* New York: Century, 1924.

Baars, Donald L. *Navajo Country: A Geology and Natural History of the Four Corners Region.* Albuquerque: University of New Mexico Press, 1995.

Barnes, Will Croft. *Arizona Place Names.* Tucson: University of Arizona Press, 1988 [1935].

Bass, William G. *The Grand Canyon in Poem and Picture.* Wickenburg, Ariz.: privately published, n.d.

Beaman, E. O. *The Cañon of the Colorado, and the Moqui Pueblos.* Cleveland: n.p., 1874.

Belknap, Buzz. *Grand Canyon River Guide.* Boulder City, Nev.: Westwater Books, 1969.

Birdseye, Claude H., and Raymond C. Moore. "A Boat Voyage Through the Grand Canyon of the Colorado." *The Geographical Review* 14 (1924): 177–96.

Bourke, John Gregory. *On the Border with Crook.* Lincoln: University of Nebraska Press, 1971 [1891].

Brian, Nancy. *River to Rim.* Flagstaff, Ariz.: Earthquest Press, 1992.

Brown, Bryan T., Steven W. Carothers, and R. Roy Johnson. *Grand Canyon Birds.* Tucson: University of Arizona Press, 1987.

Carothers, Steven W., and Bryan T. Brown. *The Colorado River Through Grand Canyon*. Tucson: University of Arizona Press, 1991.

Castañeda, Pedro de. *Narrative of the Coronado Expedition*. Washington, D.C.: U.S. Government Printing Office, 1896.

Cobb, Irvin S. *See* Schullery, Paul.

Collier, Michael. *An Introduction to Grand Canyon Geology*. Grand Canyon: Grand Canyon Natural History Association, 1980.

Colton, Harold S., and Frank C. Baxter. *Days in the Painted Desert and the San Francisco Mountains*. Flagstaff: Museum of Northern Arizona, 1932.

Crampton, C. Gregory. *Standing Up Country*. New York: Knopf, 1973.

Crumbo, Kim. *River Runner's Guide to the History of the Grand Canyon*. Boulder, Colo.: Johnson Books, 1981.

Dellenbaugh, Frederick S. *A Canyon Voyage*. Tucson: University of Arizona Press, 1984 [1908].

Dutton, Clarence E. *Tertiary History of the Grand Canyon*. Washington, D.C.: U.S. Government Printing Office, 1882.

Emrich, Duncan. *Folklore on the American Land*. Boston: Little, Brown, 1972.

Escalante, Fray Silvestre Vélez. *The Dominguez-Escalante Journal*. Salt Lake City: University of Utah Press, 1995.

Euler, Robert C. "Frederick Dellenbaugh, Grand Canyon Artist." *Journal of Arizona History* 28, no. 1 (Spring 1987): 31–46.

Field, John. *Place-Names of Great Britain and Ireland*. London: David & Charles, 1980.

Flavell, George F. *The Log of the Panthon*. Edited by Neil B. Carmony and David H. Brown. Boulder, Colo.: Pruett, 1987.

Fletcher, Colin. *The Man Who Walked Through Time*. New York: Alfred A. Knopf, 1968.

Freeman, Lewis R. *Down the Grand Canyon*. New York: Dodd, Mead, 1930.

Ghiglieri, Michael P. *Canyon*. Tucson: University of Arizona Press, 1992.

Granger, Byrd H. *Grand Canyon Place Names*. Tucson: University of Arizona Press, 1960.

Gudde, Erwin G. *California Place Names*. Berkeley: University of California Press, 1949.

Hart, John D. *A Companion to California*. Berkeley: University of California Press, 1987.

Henry, Marguerite. *Brighty of the Grand Canyon*. New York: Rand McNally, 1953.

Higgins, C. A. *Grand Cañon of the Colorado River*. Chicago: Santa Fe Railroad, 1897.

Hoffmeister, Donald. *Mammals of Arizona*. Tucson: University of Arizona Press, 1984.

Hughes, J. Donald. *The Story of Man at the Grand Canyon*. Grand Canyon: Grand Canyon Natural History Association, 1967.

Ives, Joseph C. *Report on the Colorado River of the West*. Washington, D.C.: U.S. Government Printing Office, 1861.

James, George Wharton. *The Wonders of the Colorado Desert*. Boston: Little, Brown, 1906.

———. *In and Around the Grand Canyon*. New York: Scribners, 1911.

Kolb, Ellsworth L. *Through the Grand Canyon from Wyoming to Mexico*. Tucson: University of Arizona Press, 1990 [1914].

Kroeber, A. L. *Handbook of the Indians of California*. Bureau of American Ethnology Bulletin 78. Washington, D.C.: U.S. Government Printing Office, 1925.

Krutch, Joseph Wood. *Grand Canyon*. Tucson: University of Arizona Press, 1989 [1957].

Lomax, John A. *Cowboy Songs and Other Frontier Ballads*. New York: Macmillan, 1927.

Long, Haniel. *Piñon Country*. New York: Duell, Sloan & Pearce, 1944.

Loving, Nancy J. *Along the Rim*. Grand Canyon: Grand Canyon Natural History Association, 1981.

Matthews, C. M. *Place Names of the English-Speaking World*. New York: Scribners, 1972.

McKee, Barbara H. "The Naming of the Grand Canyon." *Grand Canyon Nature Notes* 8, no. 8 (1933): 210–12.

McNamee, Gregory. *Gila: The Life and Death of an American River*. New York: Crown Publishers, 1994.

———, ed. *Named in Stone and Sky: An Arizona Anthology.* Tucson: University of Arizona Press, 1993.

Merriam, C. Hart. "Results of a Biological Survey of the San Francisco Mountain Region and Desert of the Little Colorado River, Arizona." *North American Fauna* 3: 1–136.

Muir, John. *See* Schullery, Paul.

Palmer, William R. "Indian Names in Utah Geography." *Utah Historical Quarterly* 1, no. 1 (January 1928): 5–26.

Pattie, James Ohio. *Personal Narrative.* Lincoln: University of Nebraska Press, 1984.

Peattie, Donald Culross. *A Natural History of Western Trees.* Boston: Houghton Mifflin, 1950.

Powell, John Wesley. *Canyons of the Colorado.* New York: Flood and Vincent, 1895.

Pyne, Stephen J. *Dutton's Point: An Intellectual History of the Grand Canyon.* Grand Canyon: Grand Canyon Natural History Association, 1982.

———. *Fire on the Rim.* New York: Weidenfeld and Nicholson, 1989.

Reaney, P.H. *The Origin of English Place-Names.* London: Routledge and Kegan Paul, 1960.

Schullery, Paul, ed. *The Grand Canyon: Early Impressions.* Boulder, Colo.: Pruett, 1989.

Sheldon, Charles. *The Wilderness of the Southwest.* Neil B. Carmony and David Brown, eds. Salt Lake City: University of Utah Press, 1993.

Sheridan, Thomas E. *Arizona: A History.* Tucson: University of Arizona Press, 1995.

Spamer, Earle E. *Bibliography of the Grand Canyon and Lower Colorado River.* Grand Canyon: Grand Canyon Natural History Association, 1990.

Stegner, Wallace. *Beyond the Hundredth Meridian: John Wesley Powell and the Second Opening of the West.* Boston: Houghton Mifflin, 1954.

Stewart, George R. *American Place-Names.* New York: Oxford University Press, 1960.

Stone, Julius F. *Canyon Country*. New York: G. P. Putnam's Sons, 1932.

Taylor, Isaac. *Words and Places*. London: J. M. Dent, 1911.

Thrapp, Dan L. *Encyclopedia of Frontier Biography*. Glendale, Calif.: A. H. Clark, 1988.

Thybony, Scott. *Guide to Hiking the Grand Canyon*. Grand Canyon: Grand Canyon Natural History Association, 1994.

Van Cott, John W. *Utah Place Names*. Salt Lake City: University of Utah Press, 1990.

Wallace, Robert. *The Grand Canyon*. New York: Time-Life Books, 1972.

Zeveloff, Samuel I. *Mammals of the Intermountain West*. Salt Lake City: University of Utah Press, 1988.

Zwinger, Ann Haymond. *Downcanyon*. Tucson: University of Arizona Press, 1995.

ABOUT THE AUTHOR

Gregory McNamee is the author of *Blue Mountains Far Away: Journeys into the American Wilderness* (Lyons Press, 2000), *Gila: The Life and Death of an American River* (Crown Publishers, 1995; University of New Mexico Press, 1998), *A Desert Bestiary* (Johnson Books, 1996), and many other books. He is a contributing editor to *The Bloomsbury Review,* a columnist for *The Hollywood Reporter,* a consultant and contributor to the *Encyclopaedia Britannica,* and a regular contributor to many other publications in the United States and abroad. For more information, visit his website (www.gregorymcnamee.com).